LIVING SLOWER

Simple Ideas to Eliminate Excess
and Make Time for What Matters

MERISSA A. ALINK

BakerBooks

a division of Baker Publishing Group
Grand Rapids, Michigan

© 2022 by Merissa Alink

Published by Baker Books
a division of Baker Publishing Group
PO Box 6287, Grand Rapids, MI 49516-6287
www.bakerbooks.com

Printed in the United States of America

Library of Congress Cataloging-in-Publication Data
Names: Alink, Merissa, author.
Title: Living slower : simple ideas to eliminate excess and make time for what matters / Merissa A. Alink.
Description: Grand Rapids, MI : Baker Books, a division of Baker Publishing Group, [2022] | Includes bibliographical references.
Identifiers: LCCN 2021041026 | ISBN 9781540901637 (paperback) | ISBN 9781540902030 (casebound) | ISBN 9781493434022 (ebook)
Subjects: LCSH: Storage in the home. | Orderliness.
Classification: LCC TX309 .A45 2022 | DDC 648/.8—dc23
LC record available at https://lccn.loc.gov/2021041026

The author is represented by the William K. Jenson Literary Agency.

Baker Publishing Group publications use paper produced from sustainable forestry practices and post-consumer waste whenever possible.

22   23   24   25   26   27   28   7   6   5   4   3   2   1

LIVING
SLOWER

To my wonderful husband and children.
I can't imagine going through this life without
each one of you. Everything I do in life is for you,
including writing this book.

To everyone who believed in and supported me
while I worked through not only this book but this
process, I'm so thankful for the place that
each of you holds in my life.

Contents

Contents

one

Our (Not So) Simple Story

always wanted to live a simple life. As a carefree young girl growing up on the South Dakota prairie, I wanted nothing more than to run around barefoot in the warm summer sun or to pack a picnic and enjoy it by a creek somewhere in the Black Hills. I was born with a longing for freedom, and my heart pumped that longing through my veins. I wanted to chase that freedom and live the life of my dreams.

In my teen years, I needed to begin making some decisions about which college to attend. My heart wanted to be lying in the sunshine reading books, writing books, and somewhere down the line, raising babies to be just as wild and free as my own soul was. But my brain told me no, that's not practical. When one grows up, one must go to a good school and then get a good job and have a wonderful career. Or at least that's what my family and my culture told me, and that was the direction I was encouraged toward.

After that, if it worked out, I could have some babies, but whatever I did, I needed to be successful. The opposite of success is failure, and I didn't want to be a failure. So, successful I would be.

However, at sixteen, I met the boy of my dreams. I didn't know it at the time, and neither did he. We were both working at Target. He was a cart attendant, and I worked in customer service. He claims that I never paid attention to him because of his lowly job status. The truth was, my head was stuck in the clouds and I didn't have time for boys. They would be a part of my future, but they weren't included in my short-term goals. I needed to go to college and get that good career first.

I picked a good school and started on a path that I didn't necessarily want to be on but that, I was told, would be best for my future. I didn't stop to think about why society knew better than I did what would be best for my future. I just went along with it and decided I must not be smart enough to know what I should be doing. I would let others decide that for me.

I wanted what everyone—my family, my coworkers, my friends, society—told me I should want: to lead a successful life. But I never stopped to think about what success meant to me. Even worse, I never stopped to truly ask God if that version of success was where He wanted me to be. What did He want from me? Who did God create Merissa to be? I wish I'd asked that sooner. But then, maybe if I had, I wouldn't be writing this book.

I made it through one whole year of college. I wasn't a bad student. I actually excelled in all my classes. But I had no drive. College was not my dream; it was someone else's.

My dream was to write and to raise a family. I didn't need college to accomplish those goals.

Married Life

The boy I met working at Target was persistent. He finally asked for my phone number when I was eighteen, and the next few months went by in a blur. We discovered we were basically the same person but in two different bodies, and we wanted to spend the rest of our lives together. So, on a windy day in September, nine months after he asked for my phone number, we were married.

At that point, I was done with school. I decided that I'd skip ahead from the career plan and start the family plan instead. In the meantime, I wanted to be the best wife I could be.

When I was growing up, I was taught many skills that some would consider to be old-fashioned. I was cooking full meals by the time I was ten. I knew how to sew, weave baskets, kill a rattlesnake, keep a good garden, and preserve my harvest by canning. When my husband and I got married, I wanted to be able to do all these things for my household. I wanted us to have the very best garden and to be as self-sustaining as we could be, mainly because I loved doing those things. But this almost turned into a competition with myself. I taught myself how to make many things that one would normally buy from the store—ketchup, candy bars, and anything else I could think of.

Unfortunately, things didn't go exactly as I had planned after we got married. I forgot about this little thing called money and that when you are nineteen, you don't usually have a whole lot of it. In my first book, *Little House Living: The Make-Your-Own Guide to a Frugal, Simple, and Self-Sufficient Life*, I share how my husband and I went from totally broke to pulling ourselves up by our bootstraps and being able to buy our first home.[1] We'd hit rock bottom, and there was nowhere to go but up.

All the trial and error of making things, growing things, living frugally, and everything in between turned into a blog. Because our first home was a little green house on ten acres and I had nicknamed it "Little House on the Prairie," what better name to call the blog than *Little House Living*? I shared how we were living frugally and simply in our little house out on that South Dakota prairie. My book and my blog featured all kinds of ideas on how to "make your own" everything, from shampoo to taco seasoning.

However, in those first few years of marriage, I was always in a state of anxiety or depression, and I couldn't figure out why. My body wasn't very healthy, but I was working harder at life than ever before. Things should have been wonderful, right? We were working our way toward the American Dream! I worked at a small retail store, and my husband worked as a debt collector. In those early days, my version of simpler and slower living was to try to make as much money as we could so we could have the things we wanted: a nice house and a good future. For me, that was the American Dream: to have everything we wanted or needed and to be able to do the things we wanted to do.

I still wasn't asking God what He wanted from my life or if we were on the path He wanted us to be on. I guess I just figured this was a good path, and I didn't see how there could be anything wrong with it. My theory was that if I wasn't working this hard or trying to do all the things I could possibly do, I would be classified as lazy.

Growing a Family

After about three years of marriage, our baby plan wasn't really working out. We had both wanted a big family, but it seemed God didn't have the same plan we had—at least not the way we thought it was supposed to go. We decided that in the meantime we would be foster parents. We wanted to care for children, and we thought this would be a good way to do it until God decided to make us parents.

We had a few short-term placements before our first long-term one. This baby came to us straight from the hospital, which was rare for a foster child through the state. The first time I saw him, I thought he was the tiniest thing I'd ever seen. I was terrified to pick him up with the social worker there. What if I broke him? Of course, I finally held him and felt such an odd little spark between us. Not something I'd felt with the other children we'd had in our care prior to this child. After a tumultuous thirteen months with him, we stood in a courtroom as a judge declared him to be our little boy forever.

It was totally unexpected after the trials we had been through with him and the state, but nevertheless God delivered our first child to us, and we were finally parents. Not in the way we had expected, but that didn't matter to us. I remember sitting in the social services office going through the baby's paperwork before court—something all parents must do before they adopt through the state—and having an overwhelming feeling that God did not want us to have children biologically because He knew there were other children out there who needed to be in our family. And I was at complete peace with that.

By the time my husband and I were twenty-four, our lives looked a bit more different. We were a family of three but still trying to live the American Dream. I was going to give this little boy the best start in life that he could possibly have, even if it killed me to do it, because I believed that I needed to give him the world—and more. At this point, I was still fairly unhealthy and dealing with anxiety, but I didn't stop to question it. I just thought it must be normal, and I moved on with life.

Freedom in Christ

My husband and I had been meeting with the same in-home church group since we got married. Even though I'd been raised in a typical evangelical church, my husband preferred that we meet with a group from the church that he'd grown up in and that all his family attended. After I attended a few of the services, I decided that was fine. I wanted to be a good wife and not rock the boat. And a good wife went to church with her husband. Besides, they were teaching straight from the Bible, so there couldn't be anything wrong with that, right?

After going with him for four years, I couldn't take it anymore. I didn't understand it at the time, but life was weighing on me. I told my husband I could no longer go to church with him. I had a need for perfection, but no matter how perfect I tried to be, I just couldn't achieve my goals. The drive for perfection within the group was more than I could handle, and my anxiety was through the roof. There were so many things I was expected to do that I continually failed at: I needed to dress right at all times; I needed to speak a certain way; I needed to raise my child in ways I didn't feel comfortable with.

I may have been a fairly "good" girl in the general sense of the word—I never smoked, drank, ran with the wrong crowd, etc.—but my soul is wild, not made for meaningless traditions, and it longed for freedom. I knew that my freedom was found in Christ, and something was telling me that the church I was attending didn't believe that. My husband continued to attend without me, and I decided to go back to my old church alone with our little baby.

Not long after I stopped attending church with my husband, I started to question a few things I had heard in his group. I was not prepared for what I found. From document after document, testimony after testimony sharing the true motives behind the "church," I realized that my husband was in what I defined as a cult.

A cult can mean many different things, but a basic definition of the word *cult* could be a religious system that has particular unorthodox customs. A Christian cult, such as this one, may seem to follow most of the traditional Christian beliefs, but it often denies certain fundamental Christian truths while still claiming to be a Christian organization. For example, the members of this group do not believe that Jesus is truly our Savior. Instead, they believe He came to be the perfect example of how we should live while on this earth. They also deny the teaching of the Trinity and do not believe that Jesus was equal to God.

After coming to this realization, I dug into true biblical doctrine and immersed myself in studying what the Bible actually says versus what the group claimed and believed. What I learned was that Satan can twist something that is actually far removed from the truth into something that seems incredibly innocent. As someone who had been a believer for over twenty years, I felt like I should have seen this group for what it was from the beginning. This seemed like a major failure in my life, and I felt ashamed that my eyes had been closed to the truth for as long as they were. At the time, I had no idea that God was using this whole experience to shape my future and the future of our family.

A New Start

A year after I left the group, my husband was miraculously shown the truth that lives only in Jesus and was able to come out of the group he had known his whole life. He had been praying for truth and honestly seeking answers to his questions ever since I had left the group. Whenever we talked and I asked him questions, he realized he did not have a strong answer for why he believed what he did. He began to look for answers in the Bible to truly discover what he believed and why. What he actually discovered was that he had been seriously misled by the leaders in the group. While the verses the group used were in the Bible, my husband found that they had been taken completely out of context to shape the beliefs of those in the group.

Of course, when a group believes that they are the only way to heaven and you have suddenly chosen to leave that path, they no longer want anything to do with you. As soon as it became known that my husband had renounced the group and was now a born-again Christian, we were excommunicated. We'd walk into the grocery store and see people we'd known for years, and they would turn around and walk away from us without saying a word. For a young couple still trying to make our start in the world, it was heartbreaking. We both knew that what we had done was right and that, with the knowledge we had, there was no going back, but it was still hard to lose all the friendships we thought we had gained during the early years of our marriage. We quickly learned that there was a price to pay for being a follower of Jesus.

We decided that the best thing for us to do was start over. In 2013, we moved across the state and settled down on another small acreage of land with our young son. Not long after, in 2014, we were chosen to be the parents of another sweet little boy through a private adoption, and we were overjoyed. We moved again to a larger house and kept chasing that American Dream. The house we moved into was just beautiful. It was on eight acres and had a huge barn, bedrooms for everyone, and a guesthouse. From the lovely wraparound porch, I could take in the yard, which looked like a park.

We started our own coffee shop in the small town nearby. We loved having a business and being around people. All that time, I kept thinking that I must do everything to give these boys the best start they could possibly have in life. I started homeschooling our oldest, and we made sure we were taking plenty of vacations and doing all the things we thought we needed to do. Our days were filled with special toys, extravagant crafts, and unique outings. Never mind the fact that I was trying to work two full-time jobs—blogging and running the coffee shop—while also trying to be a full-time mom and wife. In 2017, during everything else that was going on, we adopted a sweet little girl through another private adoption.

My health had improved since we had gotten out of the cult, but it still wasn't great. I was so tired by lunchtime that I would put the kids down for a nap and have to take one myself. I couldn't even make it through the afternoon without a decent nap. But I still felt so strongly that I must do everything—so I kept doing it. I was also still producing most of our food with my garden, and I'd take on any extra task that was thrown my way. Oh, and did I mention that our children have special needs? That's right: I was taking one or the other to therapy multiple times a week on top of everything else.

That's just what a good mom does, right? She overextends and stretches herself in any way she can in order to give her children the whole world. Society seemed to be pressing in on me and telling me that I had to do certain things and act certain ways and that my children should be the reason for my existence. Or, at least, that's what I believed.

Giving Up

One day a call came that I didn't expect. My childhood best friend, the one who had been my neighbor when I was little and who had still stayed in touch—even if it wasn't often—after we had grown up and gone off in different directions, had passed away from cancer at the age of twenty-seven. He was just a month older than I was. I couldn't believe it. Twenty-seven-year-olds are not supposed to get cancer, and they aren't supposed to die from it. Or, at least, that is what I kept telling myself as I sat at his funeral, almost too shocked to speak. I don't think I really understood just how short life was until that point.

Then things started snowballing. My doctor found something during my routine physical that shouldn't have been there. Then I found a lump that shouldn't have been there. Then I had a precancerous spot taken from my shoulder. I was also diagnosed with an autoimmune disease. Then another. In just two years, my life went from "Let's do it all" to "We have got to stop this train wreck right now." I was mad at God. I didn't understand why I was the one who had to go through all these things. I was young and should've been healthy and active! We had our dream house, an amazing business, and now three beautiful children. This was everything I always wanted, right?

I had not asked God if this was what He always wanted for me and our family. Was this the life He wanted me to be living? All wrapped up in myself, my wants, and my desires? I honestly thought during this time that I was living a simple life! My definition of living simple was doing all the things we wanted to do without much stress, being self-sufficient, and having what we thought we needed so we didn't have to need or want anymore. I really had no idea what simple living was then, even though I thought I did and was writing about it in my book and on my blog.

God told me, "You have to stop." He didn't whisper it to me, either, because I obviously wasn't listening. No, instead He allowed these experiences to get my attention: coming out of a cult, stressful health situations, life challenges. Maybe the first thing didn't work, so they just kept on coming. And you know what? It finally worked.

I finally cried out, "You have to take my hands off this life, Lord, because I'm doing nothing but driving it right into the ground." I finally admitted that my life wasn't mine and that I wasn't a very good driver anyway. My life had always belonged to God, and I had just been trying to steal it. So now, I gave it back to Him. It took me a while, but I realized I needed to give Him the wheel and truly be willing to let Him keep it. I wish it hadn't taken those circumstances to get me to understand what I needed to do, but I guess I'm a little more hardheaded than I'd like to admit.

I thought my job in life was to do everything: to be the perfect mom, to be the best wife, to give my children every opportunity they could possibly want. I believed that if I did not want to do those things, I would be a bad person and a bad mother. *I should have my children enrolled in everything that is available to them because, you never know, they might turn out to be the one to invent the next big thing. And I wouldn't want to be responsible for letting the opportunity pass them by.*

Why had I been so afraid to give God the control over my circumstances and over my children's lives? He gave them to me, didn't He? Why did I think I knew better than He did how they should be raised and all the things they should do?

Following God's Plan

After we'd been in our home for three years, I woke up in my beautiful bedroom in my big farmhouse one morning and whispered to my husband, "I think we are supposed to move." It felt like I was saying something terrible, words that should not even be uttered. How could I think about moving away from what others would perceive as the perfect life? Where would we go, and what would we do? We went back and forth for several months and finally concluded that God was asking us to go. He was asking us to move outside of our comfort zone because He had a plan for our family—it just wasn't exactly the one we had pictured.

Once I made the decision to let go, God took over immediately, and I knew I was ready to let Him. I gave Him my health, I gave Him my kids, and I gave Him our future.

Currently, we are in the process of building our own home, trying to keep costs down as much as we can. We've felt guided to a specific ministry: to share the love of Jesus with the group my husband grew up in and to provide a refuge to those who are in stressful and difficult situations (such as those who are leaving a fundamentalist group or cult, or those who are in ministry or missionary work and need a respite). We are both excited and a bit terrified to see what the future holds, but we fully trust in God's plan for our family. In a million years, this is not where I had expected things to be for us, yet here we are.

Since I've given in to God's plan, things have improved. My health is the best it's been in my adult life. All the lumps and areas of concern on my body have turned out to be benign, and I have an energy and mental clarity I haven't had since I was in high school—even though I'm chasing around three young children every day! I still struggle with autoimmune issues, but with diligence in my activity and in my diet, I've been able to get those issues under control.

We know things aren't always going to be perfect or even good, and more things will happen and go wrong. We live in a fallen world. Nothing will ever be perfect until we get to heaven. But I will tell you that life is much smoother when you let God take control and when you let Him plan your priorities.

The Rest of the Story

I started this book by sharing my full story because I want you to know that I've been where you've been, or maybe where you are now. I know you want to give your family the best life possible. I get that feeling—I think all moms do!

Even if you aren't a mom yet or don't ever want to be a mom, or if you're a grandma, an aunt, or anyone else, I know you still understand this truth. You likely want your life to be as perfect as it can be. We all want that, but we must realize that the only perfection we can have is perfection through Christ.

We will never be perfect while we are on this earth. Bad things might happen to us, and circumstances will be out of our control. But we can always find rest in the fact that if we have accepted Jesus into our lives and He is living through us, then God views us as perfect.

I am sure it's not hard to think of the last thing you did wrong. Or maybe I'm the only one who messed up today? But isn't it wonderful to think that when God looks at you, He sees you as totally and completely perfect? Thank goodness I don't have to pretend. Are you good at doing that? I know I'm not.

It's time to stop, take a breath, and ask yourself, *Am I the person God wants me to be? Are my priorities in order? Or am I working toward what someone else said should be done while I am on this earth?*

We live in a world of side hustles, school that starts at age two or three, and pressure to have all the toys that the Joneses have—plus some. The big house, the expensive cars, the boats, the exotic vacations . . . none of those things are bad in themselves. But are they what God wants for your life? Is that the life God wants for your family?

One thing I've noticed is that every time things start to get busier in my life, the first thing that goes out the window is my morning quiet time. Isn't Satan sneaky? He knows that living in a world that pushes us to do more and be more will shove God right out of the picture. We may not even realize it at first, but that just goes to show how crafty that old snake is.

I could be wrong. Perhaps your life is filled with many things that keep you busy all day long, and you are completely satisfied with the amount of time you spend with God and the amount of control He has in your life. But if you feel like everything is snowballing and you can't remember the last time you were able to sit in total peace and just listen for God's voice among the chaos of your day, this book is for you. I was just like you once. Some weeks, I'm still like you and let the busyness take control. I forget the beauty that comes from true simplicity and the richness that comes from a life lived in the slow lane.

Throughout the rest of this book, I will walk with you and share what happened when I let God take control of the pace of my life. I want to show you how you can make these changes so that you can make strides toward living in simplicity too. The topics I'll cover in the coming chapters are areas in which my family has experienced huge differences in our lives since we started living slower. I hope you are ready to fall in love with the life that God has planned for you.

two

The Benefits of Living a Slower Life

I know you are busy, but have you ever stopped to think about the toll that living a fast-paced life has on your family? We are part of a culture in which families are apart more than we are together.

When I was growing up, families seemed to do more activities together—camping, off-roading, hunting for a Christmas tree, big Sunday suppers—than we did early in our marriage and in the beginning of raising our children.

A study from NPR showed that 48 percent of families in the United States eat dinner together.[1] The same study also showed that of those families who eat dinner at home together, just 55 percent have the children eating the same food at the same table.

Not only that, but we are spending less and less time around the table. The average US resident uses one hour and eight minutes of their day eating food.[2] If you figure in three meals a day, that's twenty-two minutes per meal. Is that enough time to have a meaningful conversation around the table and to properly digest our food?

What about how we live our lives in general? Do we have enough time to do the things we want to and should get done in a day?

According to Pew Research, 84 percent of parents feel rushed every day, 36 percent feel like they spend too little time with their children, 38 percent say they spend too little time with their spouse, 53 percent say they spend too little time with friends, and 53 percent feel like they have no free time.[3] These statistics show us that we have become a generation so focused on the "end goal" that we have forgotten to live in the here and now.

Our Purpose

If you recognize yourself in some of these statistics, you are probably ready for a change. But how do we know what we want that change to look like? I think the first questions we need to ask ourselves are, *What do I want from my life?* and *What does God want from my life?*

How do we know what God wants us to do with our lives? We just ask Him. Matthew 6:33 says, "But seek first the kingdom of God and his righteousness, and all these things will be added to you." What does it look like to seek the kingdom of God first? "You shall love the Lord your God with all your heart and with all your soul and with all your mind. This is the great and first commandment. And a second is like it: You shall love your neighbor as yourself" (Matt. 22:37–39).

We were put on this earth not for ourselves but for the glory of God. God created us not because He needed us but because He wanted us. Isn't that a wonderful way to look at our Father? He didn't create us because He needed us to do anything for Him but because He truly *wanted* us! If God wanted to create only things that shouted His glory, He could have done that with just nature, animals, the galaxies, and other things. But He chose us. And He created us with a purpose. In all His wisdom, He would never have simply fashioned us into purposeless beings.

How many of us are living out our purpose? Are we truly living a life in which our top priorities are loving God and loving our neighbors? What does that even mean and look like in your life?

Obviously, God made us all unique. We all have different spiritual gifts that will help define and shape our purpose in this life, so the way we show our love for God and others might be quite different from the way the Christian next door shows theirs.

How many times have we cried out in prayer, asking God to show us His will for our lives? For me, this seems to be a frequent entry in my prayer journal. We can get so caught up in seeking God's will for our lives that we get conflicted on the little things in our day. *Is this what God wants me to make for supper? Where does God want us to go on vacation this year? If I paint my entryway this color, will it be welcoming to the strangers that God wants me to have in my home?* Then it becomes easy to get caught up in the mundane, day-to-day details of life rather than focus on the bigger picture. I'm not saying God doesn't care about the little things in life, but His will for us lies in the things He shares with us in His Word.

His Word tells us to

- love our neighbors (Mark 12:31)
- love God wholeheartedly (Matt. 22:37)
- be gentle (Gal. 5:23)
- practice self-control (Gal. 5:23)
- be peaceful (Gal. 5:22)
- practice patience (Rom. 8:25)
- be respectful (Titus 2:7)
- show mercy and kindness (Luke 6:36)

These should not be things we do out of some kind of legalistic striving for perfection—putting the law and rules, either religious or self-imposed, above the gospel—but instead they should be a by-product of our salvation and our earnest desire to love the Lord.

If we are intentional and diligent about our prayer life and the study of God's Word not only through individual reading but also from the teaching of others who have a solid faith, we will be able to better understand what God wants for us, and we will also begin to understand how to apply these things in our daily lives.

Some of us long for clear answers on specific problems, but unfortunately, we will never find a verse in the Bible that says, "This is exactly where I want you to buy a house." However, we know that if we are in constant prayer with our Father, He will give us peace in our hearts about decisions we need to make in our time here on earth.

Ultimately, we need to remember Romans 8:28: "And we know that for those who love God all things work together for good, for those who are called according to his purpose." God does not mean for harm to come to any of His children. That doesn't mean that bad or difficult things won't happen in this life—we know they do, right?—it just means that we can rest assured that God has a plan for our lives.

How Slower Living Fits into This Plan and What We Can Gain from It

Living a slower life helps us to be able to take a breath and see God's path for us more clearly, but it also has many other benefits beyond that. This section includes a list of some of the things my family as well as many of our simple-living friends have found to be benefits of this lifestyle. If you've been unsure about living a slower life until now, I hope you will read these suggestions with earnestness and envision these benefits in your life.

A Simpler, Slower Life Costs Less

Whenever our family strives to make more money to pay for more things, we always feel the weight of the stress, and it doesn't seem worth it in the end. When we bought our "perfect" house, which was the most expensive one we had purchased to date, instead of feeling happy, we felt only the burden of debt. What a joy to discover that living a simpler life can relieve a lot of financial stress! Most Americans live with a large amount of stress due to their financial situation.

- 78 percent of US workers live paycheck to paycheck.[4]
- The average monthly car payment in the US is $455.[5]

- The average American family with a credit card has over $6,270 in credit card debt.[6]

We would all like to have more of our paycheck left at the end of the month, wouldn't we? When you live a slower lifestyle, you'll focus less on competition and materialism so, generally, you will buy less and end up spending less money.

In our family, we are able to focus minimally on our financial income because our goal in life is not to gain material possessions. While we still need to earn a living to be able to pay the bills, we've found that when the focus isn't on buying the "latest and the greatest," we almost always have money left at the end of the month. We also don't have any credit cards because we've been able to balance our budget and plan for the unexpected.

Living a slower life can be a huge benefit because you can then use the money you saved to do things you've never had the money to do, like take more family road trips. Maybe living more simply will offer you the chance to take a job you enjoy more but that pays less than your current job, or you may even be able to be a stay-at-home parent, if that's what you've always wanted to be.

Living Slower Gives You the Chance to Have Better Relationships

Before my family lived a slower life, we seemed to have plenty of friendships but not many true relationships. When we were working all the time and trying to save any spare minutes for our own family, there was very little time to spend with friends and family outside of our household. Now that we've changed our focus and eliminated extra projects, chores, and work, we are able to be with others much more. We also have more opportunities to provide immediate help for someone who needs it because we aren't so busy or preoccupied. Now that we've slowed things down, we have much more time to focus on building relationships with others, enriching not only our lives but their lives as well. Plus, spending more time with friends and family is associated with better mental and physical health.[7]

As I mentioned at the beginning of this chapter, a large percentage of the US population feels like they spend too little time with their children, spouse, family, and friends. According to the US Bureau of Labor Statistics, the average parent spends only three minutes a day reading to their child.[8] When we slow down and remove some of the busyness from our lives, it frees up our time to be able to invest in those relationships. We can have more time to make phone calls, write letters, and spend quality in-person time with people we care about. When we don't put in time and communication, relationships quickly fall apart.

Less "Noise" Leads to Fewer Distractions

As someone who has a tendency to suffer from brain fog due to autoimmune issues, I can't afford to have many distractions or else I get completely derailed. Do you ever walk into a room and completely forget why you are there? Whenever that happens to me, I know I need to take a step back—both literally and figuratively—to refocus my attention. We've found that any kind of extra noise in our home distracts not only my husband and me but also our children. For this reason we've chosen to limit screens to work and school activity only. We've also chosen not to carry our cell phones with us in our home. We leave them in the kitchen and check them periodically to see if we need to call anyone back.

We've made these changes based on our personal experiences, but there are plenty of alarming statistics you should also be aware of related to these types of distractions.

- Children spend more than seven and a half hours a day in front of a screen (e.g., TV, video games, computer).[9] Common Sense Media reports that this does not include school or homework.[10]
- It takes an average of twenty-five minutes to get back on track after being distracted.[11]
- 50 percent of parents say that a mobile device interrupts their time with their children three or more times a day.[12]

Hearing the constant hum of the TV or seeing the constant chatter of social media can lead to a very distracted life. Even when we have extra time in our day, if we choose to fill it with media, we have less ability to focus on the here and now. Our children want us to be present when we are in their presence (as does everyone else around us), and it's hard to have good communication with our noses buried in our phones or while watching TV, playing video games, and such.

You Will Have Less Clutter

I'm not one of those women who enjoy spending their time cleaning their home. I just have so many things I'd rather do! Once our family started to get rid of the clutter (and to understand why we needed to do it), it became hard to stop. Our house may not have a lot of things in it, but it also doesn't require as much upkeep as a typical home. Typically, in the United States,

- The average person spends 2.5 days a year looking for things they can't find.[13]
- The average household has 300,000 items in it.[14]
- 10 percent of households rent a storage unit.[15]

Studies show that the average American spends about six hours per week cleaning their house.[16] This number does not include any organizing or moving around of clutter. Do you really want to spend your precious time during the day cleaning and organizing your material possessions?

Having less clutter by downsizing your material possessions has many benefits. My favorites are that you have less to clean (and thus spend less time cleaning), you have less to buy (no need to fill our lives with material possessions!), you become more creative in the ways you use what you have, and you spend less money on upkeep.

You Will Get to Know Yourself Better

- 21 percent of Christians do not believe that God has given them a spiritual gift.[17]
- Studies have shown that people's coworkers are better than they are at recognizing how their personality will affect their job performance.[18]

One thing I've found to be true about living slower is that you get to know yourself better because you have more time to do it. You get to know your habits, your qualities, and your shortcomings. You may even learn about new skills that you are interested in pursuing and ways that you can build up your spiritual gifts.

I love to sing. I've always known that about myself. But when our lives slowed down, I finally decided to take vocal lessons after wanting to try them for so many years. Now that I've taken the time to improve this skill, I use it to sing hymns and songs of worship to the Lord and to my children every day. I even recorded a CD of hymns to bless my Granny with, and I hope to use this skill to bless others in the future as well.

Living Slower Allows for Healthier Eating . . .

Eating healthy was not something we did early in our marriage. I could cook from scratch and make all kinds of goodies, but creating healthy meals wasn't something I was striving to do. Because of my health issues, I had to change my eating habits or continue to suffer the consequences. When I had to do this, I was thankful that our slower lifestyle allowed me to do it easily. Now I have more time to cook foods from scratch and to better plan out my meals. I even have more time to better research foods that would be best for my family and try to implement any changes we wish to make.

- Frequent family meals are associated with lower rates of depression, anxiety, substance abuse, and other issues, and higher rates of resilience and high self-esteem.[19]

- Only about one in three families regularly eat dinner together each day.[20]
- Empty calories from added sugars and solid fats contribute to 40 percent of total daily calories for two- to eighteen-year-olds, and half of these empty calories come from six sources: soda, fruit drinks, dairy desserts, grain desserts, pizza, and whole milk.[21]

I cannot stress enough the importance of having at least one sit-down, from-scratch meal each day with your family. Multiple studies have shown that it is over this mealtime that we can more easily connect as a family and have important conversations so we know what is going on in our children's lives. It's a time in our day when we can slow down together.

Spending more time over a meal not only improves family relationships but can also improve health. You don't need to make every meal together a four-course meal. But if you have more time to prepare your meal and if you focus on enjoying simpler foods, your meals can be much healthier.

. . . And Healthier Living Too

Anyone who has known me for several years has been able to see the change in my health in recent years. Some days, I look back at old pictures and think about how rough I was feeling during those times, and I am so thankful that my family took the necessary steps to live healthier.

Our family is now so much more active than we were before. Mostly because we have the time to be! When the weather is nice enough to be outside, our entire family will often hike or walk for several miles. It's been a wonderful addition to our lives because it's something we can enjoy

34

together (and often prompts great conversations), and it's something we enjoy doing with friends as well.

When we don't take the time to slow down and prioritize our health, it can take a toll on our lives in many different ways.

- The annual cost of being overweight is $524 for women and $432 for men. The annual costs for being obese are even higher: $4,879 for women and $2,646 for men.[22]
- Less than 5 percent of adults participate in thirty minutes of physical activity each day.[23]

Not only can living slower help you have more time to take care of your body and eat healthy food, but you may also find that you have more time for physical activities and exercise than you had when you were living a busy life.

Slower Living Is Less Stressful Living

- Almost every system in our body is affected by chronic stress.[24]
- 77 percent of people regularly have physical symptoms from being stressed.[25]
- Long-term stress weakens your body's immune system.[26]
- Americans spend over $300 billion each year on health care and lost workdays due to stress.[27]

When we remove stressors that are burdening us and instead focus on God and the positive things in life, our risk for chronic illness will decrease. Some of the major stressors that were affecting my body were my striving for perfection, saying yes to extra tasks when I didn't really want to or feel that I should, and trying to do too much in a short amount of time.

As you can imagine after reading through the benefits of living a slower life, your life will be less stressful when you slow it down. You can have more quality in your relationships, get out of the rat race, consume less media, take care of your body, and much more. Removing stressors from your life and learning to truly live in the richness of the life God has planned for you is a beautiful thing.

Living Slower Improves Our Walk with God

My personal walk with God barely existed early in my marriage. I wasn't often praying by myself or with my husband, and I wasn't doing any personal Bible studies. When I researched statistics about this, I found I wasn't the only one who struggled in this area.

- Fewer than one out of every five self-identified Christians (18 percent) claim to be totally committed to investing in their own spiritual development.[28]
- Only 55 percent of Christians rely heavily on prayer.[29]
- While nine out of ten American households own a Bible, only 11 percent have read it through. And only 48 percent of evangelicals read their Bible daily.[30]

When we have a busy, stressful day, reading our Bible and practicing hospitality (caring for others) may be the last things on our minds. Living a hurried life means we have less time to spend with God in prayer or in reading His Word, and when we do spend that time with Him, it's likely filled with distractions.

My husband and I are now very aware that God needs to be in the center of our relationship, so we've made more time for studying the Bible together. I am also thankful for the time I've made for my morning Bible reading. Even on the days when I don't have as much time as I would like, I'm glad for any time I've set aside to read, pray, and grow closer to my Creator. When we slow things down and become intentional about how we spend our time, we can make those things our priority.

Living Slower Allows for More Good Works

When my husband and I were striving toward the American Dream, we usually thought only of ourselves and our needs above others. If we had time to think about someone else, that was fine, but it didn't happen often since it wasn't a priority in our busy schedules. While I believe in my heart that, deep down, most Christians want to help others, it seems we often aren't making it a priority or are doing it for the wrong reasons.

- In 1993, 89 percent of Christians who had shared their faith agreed that it is a responsibility of every Christian. Today, just 64 percent say so—a 25 percent drop.[31]
- 52 percent of those who describe themselves as Christians believe that their good works will get them into heaven.[32]

When we live a fast-paced life, we simply don't have the time to spend in God's Word to see what He really wants, so we are left to come up with conclusions based on our own ideas and our own control. This can easily turn into legalism—putting the law above the greatest commands to love God and to love others.

But we know that good things come out of having a relationship with God. By talking to Him regularly and reading the messages He's sent us in His Word, good works will flow from us as a by-product of our relationship with Him. We won't just feel like we *have* to do good things; we will truly *want* to do good things.

How Do We Know It's Time to Live Slower?

This past week we had a little incident in our house. The kids were actually getting along with each other and playing nicely, both inside and outside (a miracle!). We followed our normal daily routine but included a little extra cleaning. I'd gotten off track recently because we had been trying to get as much done on the house we were building as we could before winter set in.

Even though I had tried to even out our routines and schedules, things were a little crazier than usual. We went to tuck the boys into bed and had to take away foam swords that they insisted on taking to bed with them. (If you happen to have little boys who share a room, you can likely see how this scenario was about to play out.) That should have been the end of it. It was dark in the room and time for bed. Time to snuggle in and close our eyes for the day.

But it was not to be so. My middle child lost it. A full-blown meltdown over a little toy that he couldn't even play with in the dark anyway. As we struggled to grasp the meaning behind this episode over something seemingly so small, I heard him cry, "You are just too busy!"

I asked him to come downstairs to the living room and sit on my lap. "Explain to me what you mean. Mommy is not busy," I said.

He said, "I'm not mad that you took the sword away; I'm worried that you won't remember to give it back in the morning because you are too busy!"

I spent the next fifteen minutes assuring him that I would not forget to give his toy back in the morning and reminding him that not all little boys are as lucky as he is. He has toys to play with. He gets to see both of his parents every day. We have three meals a day together. He knew these things, but reassurance is always helpful. He calmed down and trotted back off to bed where he slept soundly the rest of the night.

But was he right? In the evenings, after the loudness of the children has quieted and I can hear my thoughts again, I always take time to reflect on my day. I knew that my son was a lucky little boy—all my children are. Since my husband and I don't work for anyone else, we have the flexibility to make our own schedules and spend as much quality time with our children as we want.

But is it enough? I think our family leads a slow life, but I know there is always room for improvement. As we grow in our walk with God, our knowledge about ourselves, and our relationships with others, sometimes things have to change.

This small incident was my reminder that my routines weren't what I needed them to be or what my children needed them to be. As a mother, my children are one of my biggest priorities (behind my marriage and my relationship with

God). It's paramount that I make the necessary adjustments. In this case, I needed to add a little more one-on-one time with each of my children into my day. Not only that, but it needed to be an affirming time, a time when I could not only be with them or play with them but also encourage them and build them up.

Perhaps in your day, you have times like these. Little moments that make you stop and think, *Is this how I want to be living my life? What are the real reasons behind these actions? Are they things that I can fix or change?*

Maybe for you, they're not little moments but perhaps big ones that take your breath away and make you wonder if you are doing the right thing. Maybe you lost your job, your family is down to one income, and you wonder how to make life less stressful.

I believe we all have these times in life that cause us to stop, think, and pivot if necessary. I believe God uses these moments to teach us, rebuke us, and steer us in the right direction.

There are plenty of paths we can choose in this life that are easy to take. Living a simpler, slower life isn't necessarily one of them. It's hard to break the cycle of the constant hustle and deliberately put aside the things that are distracting us.

If we make the effort and we pray fervently, anything is possible.

three

How to Get Started

Everyone who reads this book will be starting in a slightly different place. Perhaps you feel like you've already begun to slow things down by taking some activities off your schedule and enjoying more family time. That's wonderful! And if that's the case, starting on a different area of simplifying will be best. You might even want to skip around to different chapters of this book as you feel inspired to work on those areas.

If you haven't started simplifying anything in your life yet, this chapter is for you. If your life feels chaotic, like it's about to spin out of control, I'm here for you. We are going to do this together. Take your time with each chapter. It takes time to form new habits, and that is essentially what we are doing here: trying to turn old, busy habits into richer, slower experiences.

You didn't create your currently busy life in one day, and it's going to take more than one day to create a slower lifestyle. Sit back, relax, and enjoy the ride. Half of the beauty of slowing down is realizing what you are leaving behind and understanding why you want to push ahead. Take time to consider those things as you work your way into this journey.

Focus Less on Materialism

What do you think about when you think of the word *minimalist*? Do you picture someone in a stark-white home, surrounded by nothing but a few plants? Perhaps you see them wearing a white T-shirt and jeans, trying to serve supper from a single bowl (also white) to every member of the family. "No forks anymore, kids. We only have spoons now because we are minimalists!"

Honestly, that's what I thought too when I first heard about minimalism. To some people, that is minimalism. But to our family, *minimalism* is the opposite of *materialism*. If *materialism* is being caught up in all the material possessions we can have, then *minimalism* is not caring much about any material possessions.

When we focus less on material items, a few things start to happen. First, our homes and our judgment become less cluttered by all the things we think we need to have. Second, we spend less money because we aren't trying to keep up with the latest the world has to offer. And third, when we spend less time and money chasing after material things, we have extra resources to devote to the things we really want to do and the things God is asking us to do.

I placed the chapter on decluttering and minimizing possessions (chap. 4) so early in this book because I feel that it is foundational to the rest of the things you will read about and want to do.

If you are unsure about where to start your slower-living journey, that is definitely the chapter you need to get started on and work through before tackling the rest of this book. Take time to clear out the clutter in your home and in your mind first so you can have a fresh start and be ready to start working your way through some of the more difficult things.

Carve Out a Time to Rest

There will always be a plethora of things to do, especially if you are a mom. The workload never ends! But it doesn't need to feel that way. In order to have time to rest, we need to learn to be more intentional with our time.

Chapter 12 is about rest and Sabbath, and in that chapter, I will go into detail about what those look like for my family and what they might look like for you. But for now, I want you to get into the mindset that it's okay to have a day of rest, an evening of rest, or even just an hour of rest. Rest doesn't have to mean sitting around doing nothing (although sometimes it does!); it means setting aside the stressful work for a time in order to be present and take a breath.

Life isn't going to slow down on its own anytime soon. But we can make an effort to slow it down if we choose to. As you work your way into this book, begin to consider what effect a day of rest could have on your family and your own well-being.

Create Routines and Schedules

Do your family life and daily plans seem to be completely up in the air? Are your children frustrated with you because plans change so frequently that no one ever knows what direction they are heading?

It is important to plan and implement new routines in your home so your days become smoother and flow together in a simpler way. This does *not* mean you need to schedule and plan out every minute of the day. None of my routines include exact times (besides wake-up and bedtime for the kids); they are simply a natural flow of activities we put together to make a certain task or time of day more productive and laid back.

I will go into more detail about routines and schedules in chapter 8, but for now, I want you to begin thinking about your day and which parts of it could use some improvement. Consider writing these things down in a journal or notebook if you think you might forget.

Living slower does not mean having a boring life. It just means that we are more intentional with our time. Routines and other advance planning will help you achieve this intentionality so you can fit the things you want to do into your day.

Make Time for Family and Fellowship

Spending time with our family and spending time with others in fellowship are very important in our home. (*Fellowship* here means a gathering of believers for the purpose of encouraging and building each other up.) They're so important that we've made extra provisions in our life to be able to make them happen. This past summer, we built a campsite on our property to host families who just need a place to go to rest, regroup, or have fellowship. Even though we've only had the site for less than a year, we've found it to be a wonderful way to fellowship with others.

Do you tend to struggle in your daily walk because you don't feel like you have support or encouragement from others? I used to feel that way, and I was sure it was because no one liked me, but when I took a step back, I realized I was not putting forth the effort I could have been to make those relationships happen or to build and grow them. I was too caught up in my own worries to realize that there were plenty of people around me to fellowship with; I just needed to make the time and effort for that to happen.

If you are feeling lonely or like you are not surrounded by the right people, it's time to start thinking about how you can better your relationships with family and friends, specifically friends you can have fellowship with. Later, in chapter 10, I will go into more detail about family togetherness, fellowship, and why we shouldn't be alone, but for now, I want you to begin considering the possibility of better relationships or even writing your thoughts about it in a journal. Think about the impact that having a solid group of believers to lean on and bettering your relationships with your family could have on your life.

Family togetherness is a goal that we regard highly in our home. When we spend time doing things together as a family, we build an immensely strong bond that will carry into the future and shape our children's lives. If God has given you children or someone younger to care for in any way, building a tight-knit relationship with them can be one of the most important things you do while you are on this earth. The Bible speaks many times of the importance of the relationship between an older person and a younger person.

Older women likewise are to be reverent in behavior, not slanderers or slaves to much wine. They are to teach what is good, and so train the young women to love their husbands and children, to be self-controlled, pure, working at home, kind, and submissive to their own husbands, that the word of God may not be reviled. (Titus 2:3–5)

You (and possibly you alone) are in the right place to make an impact on this young person's life. Don't waste that opportunity!

What a Week Looks Like for My Family

Although my family's daily and weekly activities change from season to season, I want to give you a peek at what a typical week in our life looks like. Keep in mind that the week I'm describing as an example represents the general flow of our weeks without any changes to our typical schedule, even though they do happen on occasion.

I share this example not so you'll feel intimidated by our schedule but so you'll feel inspired and hopefully encouraged to follow the tips you will find later in this book and start living the simpler life you've been dreaming about.

Our week begins on Sunday with church. Since I have minimized our clothing choices by decluttering, getting ready in the morning is not as hectic. We all have certain clothes we keep clean and wear only for church, which makes clothing decisions very easy.

After church, we either come home or head out to do a family activity. Each Sunday (our Sabbath day) looks a little different for our family, but we always spend it together not doing our normal daily work. On weeks when the weather is nice, we might go for a hike, go fishing, or go off-roading.

On not-so-nice Sundays, we might play board games or have fellowship with another family.

On Monday, we are back to the typicalness we go through four days a week (Monday, Tuesday, Thursday, and Friday). As we do every day, we follow our morning routine before we really start the day. (Our morning routine consists of time with God, getting dressed, and having breakfast. See chapter 8 for more.) After our morning routine, either my husband or I will work (depending on the day) and the other spouse will start school with the kids. This lasts about an hour and a half.

Once school is done for the day, the kids help with chores if needed. This is also the time we work on laundry or any other pressing household chores that should be done that day. The rest of the morning is spent working on any projects we'd like to work on while the kids either help or play.

After lunch, we have about an hour of quiet time. This allows the kids to rest, read, or just have some general calmness in their day, and it gives the parents a bit of a break as well. We usually use this time to catch up on work or continue working on whatever project we are currently doing.

After quiet time, the kids play together either inside or outside, or we head out to play with friends. At some point in the afternoon, the working parent finishes their work, and we as parents work on anything together that we need to get done that day. One parent also starts supper.

In the evening, we follow our bedtime routine after supper. (Bedtime and morning routines can both be found in chapter 8.) After the kids are in bed is our time together as parents to connect, talk through our day, and make plans for the coming day.

Perhaps Mondays, Tuesdays, Thursdays, and Fridays sound like rather boring days, but during just one single weekday, we can easily keep our home tidy, have our school lessons, fellowship with friends, have time together as a family, talk to God, spend time on work and ministry, and build our connection as a couple.

Wednesdays and Saturdays are slightly different. We do school only four days a week, and Wednesday is our day off. This is the day that we have the opportunity to go to town and get groceries or supplies if we need to and/or visit family. Unless the weather is poor, this is always our plan for Wednesdays, right after our morning routine. I've also detailed our routine specifically for this day in chapter 8.

Saturday is our day to catch up on anything we did not get done during the week, or it is an open day to volunteer if we are able to. In general, though, Saturdays are spent at home tying up our loose ends for the week and preparing for whatever we plan to do on Sunday.

This is how a typical week goes for us. Not all days are perfect and some have bumps in them, but in general this is what our week looks like.

Does our week look the way you expected it to? Perhaps you thought slower living looked like sitting around in a rocking chair for most of the day, working on knitting. (Not that knitting isn't a worthy hobby and can't have a place in your week!)

Although we live what I would consider to be a slower life, our lives are not boring in the least. We still have jobs (although we are self-employed), we still have full days, we still have chores. The difference is that we do the things we do because we *want* to be doing them. We've given up certain other activities so we have time and money to do what God is asking us to do. Yes, my husband could go out and get a full-time, typical job and we'd have more money for nicer things, but we've chosen not to take that road. Instead, we both work part-time from home, enough to pay the bills and give us time to run a ministry.

Some life choices aren't easy, and there are sacrifices to be made. We've chosen to sacrifice many things that might be on the typical American Dream agenda so our family can live this lifestyle. I never view these as sacrifices though, only as steps we needed to take to live our life the way God wants us to live it and to raise our children the way He wants us to raise them. I view it as a blessing that God has opened my eyes and helped give my husband and me discernment about what we should and shouldn't be doing. I'm also thankful we serve a God of patience, because there have been several times when I've felt I needed to fight back about a choice I wanted to make that God did not seem to want for our life. In the end, I know that His will is always what I want to serve, but I wouldn't be honest if I didn't tell you that sometimes my stubborn head gets in the way!

Prepare for Your Journey

If you feel like you already have some of the topics in this book down and want to jump ahead, you can skip around to the chapters you want to work on first. However, I recommend reading the chapters of this book in order. It's good to start with a baseline and build your way up, and that's the way I've written this book. You don't need to feel overwhelmed. Take the reading slowly so you can really take in the message and plan to make the necessary changes.

Appendix 2 contains a list of many journaling prompts that go along with the topics in this book. Even if you aren't someone who regularly keeps a journal, I recommend having one to keep track of your ideas and thoughts.

Right now, start with your hopes, aspirations, and wishes. What does your ideal week look like? What activities would you be doing? What would you like to do that you feel you can't fit into your week right now? Would it be spending more time with friends or family? Would it be having more time for a specific volunteer or ministry position? Or is it something more revolutionary, like being able to stay at home full-time with your children or taking a different job that pays much less but is something you've always had the heart to do?

Take your time to think through these questions, maybe even more time than you feel you need. Do not reflect on these in terms of the American Dream as you or anyone else defines it. You won't find anything in this book about how to build wealth or have a pool in your backyard. This reflection should be about the deepest desires of your heart.

After you contemplate these questions, pray, then pray some more. If you haven't already, ask God about the direction He'd like you to take with everything that has been on your heart. Then take it further: Ask others to pray for and along with you. You don't need to give them specifics if you don't want to (but you can if you want to!); just tell them you are considering slowing down some parts of your life and you want to be quiet enough to hear what God would like you to do.

Psalm 37:4–5 says, "Delight yourself in the LORD, and he will give you the desires of your heart. Commit your way to the LORD; trust in him, and he will act."

Don't be frustrated when you don't feel like you have a clear answer. Some answers come with time, and some answers never come at all. We may not see our earthly purpose until someday when we are in heaven. But I do believe God gives us desires in our hearts, and He will be pleased with us if we follow those paths in our lives that fit with His commandments. Matthew 22:34–39 says,

> But when the Pharisees heard that he had silenced the Sadducees, they gathered together. And one of them, a lawyer, asked him a question to test him. "Teacher, which is the great commandment in the Law?" And he said to him, "You shall love the Lord your God with all your heart and with all your soul and with all your mind. This is the great and first commandment. And a second is like it: You shall love your neighbor as yourself."

I love the simplicity that these verses bring to mind, and I'm so thankful that Jesus summed everything up for us to present it to us in this simple way.

Love God with everything you have.

Love others as much as you love yourself.

If we keep those two things in mind as we work on our own slower-living journey, can you imagine the life God will have us lead?

If we truly love God with everything we have and talk to Him on a regular basis, what kind of impact will He have in our life? What difference do you think that will make for our actions?

I'm guessing you would do a lot to keep yourself safe, healthy, and happy. Loving yourself doesn't have to be a vanity thing; it's something all of us do without thinking. Can you imagine what might happen to this world if we genuinely loved others as much as we love ourselves? If we became as concerned with their well-being as we are with our own?

I'm excited to dive into these next chapters with you, into our journey of slower and simpler living. I know you are here for a purpose and you are going to make an impact on the world around you, whether it will be on your own family or on a more global scale. We all have it inside us to live the way God wants us to live, but first we must slow down and let go of all the things we've gotten caught up with. We need to let our walls fall down and be willing to try something different from the path we've been on. The way might be difficult, but the rewards will be well worth it.

> Sell your possessions, and give to the needy. Provide yourselves with moneybags that do not grow old, with a treasure in the heavens that does not fail, where no thief approaches and no moth destroys. For where your treasure is, there will your heart be also. (Luke 12:33–34)

> And let us not grow weary of doing good, for in due season we will reap, if we do not give up. (Gal. 6:9)

> Whatever you do, work heartily, as for the Lord and not for men, knowing that from the Lord you will receive the inheritance as your reward. You are serving the Lord Christ. (Col. 3:23–24)

> And without faith it is impossible to please him, for whoever would draw near to God must believe that he exists and that he rewards those who seek him. (Heb. 11:6)

four

Decluttering and Minimizing

I have never considered myself a hoarder, but my mom might tell you differently. When I was little, I loved to play with stuffed animals—Beanie Babies and Pound Puppies to be exact. I loved those little creatures and would set up elaborate towns and play dramatically with my little fuzzy babies. But they didn't make many accessories to go with the stuffed animals, so I decided I would take this task upon myself. I made all my little creatures clothes out of scraps of fabric, books and play money out of construction paper, necklaces out of beads and ribbon, and furniture out of old candy boxes. You name it—I probably used it to create something for my stuffed animals.

Those years were incredibly beneficial to my grown-up life because they helped me learn to use the resources I've been given or have on hand to be creative. Just last year, I pulled out the boxes of those Beanie Babies and Pound Puppies so I could start giving them to my own children. Yes, I saved all my dolls, toy horses, stuffed animals, and Barbies— because I wanted to have a little girl who would play with them someday.

And guess what I found in those boxes with the stuffties (as my children call them)? All my handmade accessories. I pulled out container after container of tiny pieces of paper, pretend coins, fabric scraps, beaded things—all the trinkets I had made for them and deemed important enough to keep all these years. Truth be told, I had no idea that any of those were still in there. All I knew was that I dragged along all these boxes of my childhood toys every time we moved, never even bothering to look inside, just thinking I needed to save everything in them for "someday." I wanted my children to have the toys, but did they need every scrap of paper, every old Dots candy box, or every little bead that I considered precious back in the day? No, I want them to be creative in their own way.

After all the time, effort, money, and space I used moving around all those boxes, in the end, I needed and wanted only a couple of things out of them: the few useful items that my children would love and be able to play with for many years to come. I didn't need to keep all the "baggage" that came with them, but until I actually decided it was time to declutter and minimize, I didn't even know it was still there.

Are you keeping things that you really don't need? How much time and effort and space are you allowing for items that may not have any value in your life? Decluttering and minimizing can be a hard topic for some people to deal with. Many of you were raised with the same mindset I was.

We believe we should save things for later in case we need them or in case we may be able to repurpose them. I believe wholeheartedly in frugality and living within your means, but maybe we've been saving things just to save them, not because we will *need* them.

If you picture a minimalist as someone who keeps only a single cup and plate per person in the household or someone who chooses to sit on the floor instead of on a comfy couch, my family would not qualify. We're not that austere. We're comfortable minimalists. We don't have much more than we need, but we do have more than a traditional minimalist might have. Much of our "extra" comes from the fact that I love to garden and can, and if you are also into those activities, you know that it's impossible to minimize canning equipment and jars. No, our family is able to enjoy just the amount of possessions we need to work toward our life and family goals without accumulating so much that we are overwhelmed with clutter. I think that's a healthy balance to have and a good goal to keep in mind while you work through your own decluttering journey.

Why We Need to Minimize Possessions

While each person has their own reasons for wanting to minimize worldly items, these are some of my favorites:

- You will spend less money on stuff because you simply won't buy as much anymore. I'm a very frugal person and love to save money when I can. When you are buying things that aren't necessary (e.g., buying things just to buy them, buying things to keep up with the Joneses, buying things because you can't find the thing you already have), you are wasting money that could be put to better use.

- You will spend less time cleaning because you will have fewer things to clean and put away. I love this reason to declutter because I don't really like to spend my time cleaning! Who does? There are way more fun and important things we can spend our precious time on in this world besides dusting a shelf of trinkets.

- Overall, you will spend less time thinking about material possessions. This is a big one. Life is short. God put us here in a specific time for a specific purpose, and I highly doubt that purpose is to spend our time pondering worldly items. Hebrews 13:5 reminds us, "Keep your life free from love of money, and be content with what you have, for he has said, 'I will never leave you nor forsake you.'"

Once you start downsizing your possessions in a major way, it will feel so good to get rid of all the physical and mental clutter that you won't want to stop. It is completely freeing. We were not made to be materialistic beings. We were made to have our minds set on things above (see Col. 3:2). When you begin to care less about the things you own, you will free your mind to be able to focus on other things that you didn't have time to focus on before. Maybe those are your children, your spouse, your friendships, your walk with God, or even your hobbies or spiritual gifts. What are your worldly possessions holding you back from?

Your life is important. It is significant. Your life is unique, and you have a purpose. Our time on earth is short, so we must spend each day remembering these truths and holding on to God, who loves us. He doesn't want us to be bogged down with things that are ultimately insignificant.

How to Get Started

The most overwhelming part of decluttering and minimizing possessions is getting started. Where should you start? How do you start? I want you to keep in mind a few important things:

- All your clutter did not happen in a day.
- Your clutter will not be gone in a day.
- It will take several cycles of decluttering over time to get to where you want to be.

The first time I did a major declutter was about five years after my husband and I were married, when we were moving from our three-thousand-square-foot house into a four-hundred-square-foot RV. I started the decluttering process about four months before the move and worked little by little each week until we had few enough possessions to make the move but enough to be satisfied with what we had left.

If you are a list person like me, you will like this next part. I'm going to outline what a good decluttering session should look like before I dive into the details. Your own personal decluttering journey may vary a little based on the size of your household and the amount of possessions you own. But remember, all of this will happen over a period of at least a month, if not longer. Take your time so you can get to all the areas you want to and not feel like you "just need to get through it all."

A Good Room-by-Room Decluttering Cycle

Here's the best order, based on my experience, for moving around your home while working through a decluttering cycle.

1. Kitchen
2. Living room / dining room
3. Bathrooms
4. Bedrooms
5. Closets
6. Garage
7. Anywhere else

This order tends to work best because it's based on prioritizing first the rooms that are used the most.

Plan for Each Room

1. Start each room when you have at least several days to work through it. Pull out everything that's in the room and place it in the middle of the floor. There should be nothing left in any of the cupboards or dressers. (If there is a closet in the room, save the closet items for later in your decluttering cycle.) This visual of seeing everything you own is incredibly important.

2. As you go through the items in the room, make a few different piles: one for items to donate, one for

items to trash/recycle, and one to keep. Do this rather quickly, and make decisions based on your initial gut feelings.

3. Once you have gone through everything in the room and have it all sorted into piles, remove the donation and trash piles to make more space in the room.

4. Now you should be left with all the items you decided to keep. Leave these things for another day. You will need more time, brainpower, and a fresh set of eyes to sort through what you have left.

5. After a day or two, when you've had time to think and your decisions are not fueled by emotions, go back through the "keep" pile. Look at each item carefully and ask yourself the decluttering questions in the section below.

6. Remove the items you find you no longer need after asking these questions.

7. Gather the items that you have decided to keep. If you cannot decide where in your home an item will go, reconsider keeping it. Any items that don't have a "home" are always going to cause clutter.

8. Finally, look at the furniture in the room. Is it in good shape? Is it being used? Does it have a purpose? Do you find it beautiful? Furniture can be a huge source of clutter. Remove any unused furniture and give it away or sell it.

9. Take a step back and look at your fully cleaned and refreshed room. Be proud of what you have accomplished!

Once you have cleaned out a room, you can move on to the next one on your list. But keep in mind that once you finish the entire cycle of rooms, you should probably start over and go through them again. You can repeat the decluttering cycle until you are happy with the amount of possessions you have left, no matter how many cycles it takes to get to that point.

Decluttering Questions

With each item you are planning to keep, you should ask yourself a series of questions to decide if it's really worth holding on to. You may be keeping it for a nonessential purpose. Here are the questions I always ask.

Am I using this now? When was the last time I used this?

If I can't remember the last time I used an item, it's time for it to go. Some items, especially clothing, have seasonal use, but they are an exception to the rule. If you are keeping something that you don't use just for the sake of keeping it, it's probably time to let it go.

Is this item sentimental? Why?

Items with sentimental value are probably the most difficult type to deal with. I held on far too long to sentimental items, such as the homemade accessories for my stuffed animals, before I decided to go through them and ask the hard questions. Even if an item is sentimental, you don't want it in your home if it causes you extra work (e.g., caring for the item, cleaning the item, etc.). Normally it's not really the item itself that holds the sentimental value; it's the memories we have attached to it. Consider taking a picture of the item and then writing the story of the memory associated with it. That way the story and memory can always be part of your life, even though you decided to let go of the physical item that goes with it.

However, if it is a sentimental item that should stay in the family, ask if another family member is willing to care for it. It is okay to find a new home for the item if you simply don't have the time to take care of it (cleaning, dusting, maintaining it, etc.) or the space to keep it. You are under no obligation to keep material items just because someone else wants you to (see the next question).

Ultimately, as believers, we must remember that we are to be laying up treasure in heaven, not on this earth. While it's okay to have memories and stories to pass along to our children, we don't have to pass along material things if we don't want to. None of the items will go with us to heaven. This is revealed in Matthew 6:19–21: "Do not lay up for yourselves treasures on earth, where moth and rust destroy and where thieves break in and steal, but lay up for yourselves treasures in heaven, where neither moth nor rust destroys and where thieves do not break in and steal. For where your treasure is, there your heart will be also."

Am I keeping this out of obligation? Would it cause guilt to get rid of it?

Sometimes these questions go along with the previous sentimental value questions, or the sense of obligation can be for an entirely different reason. In our society, people tend to give a lot of gifts. Most of us end up with quite a few things each year that we don't really use but that were gifts from people who are special to us. This can make them difficult to get rid of.

Here is what you need to know: You are under no obligation to keep anything that was given to you. Repeat that statement and memorize it before you start decluttering. Just because your best friend gave you a set of cute coffee mugs for your birthday three years ago doesn't mean you need to keep them. If you don't use them and they are taking up extra space in your home, it's time to part with them. This is when we need to remember that it truly is the thought that counts when it comes to gift giving. When my little boys bring me a handful of dandelions, I don't preserve them so I can hold on to them forever. I put them in a little cup of water for the day, express my gratitude at their thoughtfulness, and then I let the flowers go at the end of the day or by the next morning.

Your friend or aunt or cousin or mom does not want you to keep something they gave you if it is going to cause you any kind of stress, especially clutter stress. They will understand if you enjoy those things for only a short time and then pass them along to someone else. If they don't understand this and continually ask about an item they gave you, that is their problem, not yours. No one else gets to decide what comes into your home and what stays except for you.

How much time does it take me to care for this item?

This is a great question to ask while decluttering because it comes back to the heart of why you are minimizing your possessions in the first place. When you look at the items in your "keep" pile, are you seeing things that take a lot of your time to care for and don't seem to be worth the effort? I'm talking about things that require extra dusting or cleaning, or maybe high maintenance items, like clothing that needs to be dry-cleaned. Ask yourself if you really want to continue to care for this item if you keep it. Is it more work than it is worth? Decide if it deserves a place in your new slower, simpler life.

Could someone else use this item more than I can?

I didn't start asking myself this question until a few years ago. I was keeping some things with a plan to use them someday, but "someday" never seemed to come. One day, I was reading a book that mentioned the idea that someone else could possibly use, or may even need, the items that were sitting in the back of my closet. Why was I holding on to those baby clothes that I was never going to use again? Someone somewhere could really use those things for their baby, but instead, I was letting them sit in the back of my closet, perhaps until the colors faded and the elastic was no good. What use would those items be then? A few months later, I was reading through the book of Acts and came upon this verse about the behavior of the early disciples, and it really struck my heart: "And they were selling their possessions and belongings and distributing the proceeds to all, as any had need" (Acts 2:45).

The early Christians had an amazing thing going. They wanted equality among one another, and clearly some were more blessed with possessions than others. They chose to give away what they had so all could benefit and be taken care of. This verse refers to selling items and giving the money away, which is something we can do with our unused possessions. But we can also give the possessions away to others who have a need. This question was something I struggled with when it came to an item that was both sentimental *and* that I was keeping for "someday." When I got to the point where I knew in my heart that God did not want us to add any more children to our family, I still held on to boxes and boxes of baby clothes for at least a year. Eventually I made the decision to give them all away to those who could use them. I knew it was selfish of me to keep them stored up in the closet with the elastic and the colors wearing out when someone else could've been using them right then.

Does this item have a home within my home?

This is the final question you should ask yourself about any item you decide to keep. It may have passed all the other tests and questions, but if you simply don't have a space for it within your home, it's going to continue to add to the clutter. Find a home for every single thing you keep, or give it away.

Extra Tips for Room-by-Room Decluttering

- If you don't have enough space in the room you're working on to place everything on the floor, designate another room in your house to be the "decluttering zone."
- When decluttering kids' rooms, get them involved. They need to learn to make decisions about what they keep in their space, and they need to learn the cost of keeping too many material possessions.

- When decluttering clothing, be careful to keep only what is actually used. Keep a few extra things for children, since they tend to play hard in their clothes. Don't keep clothing for yourself that is too big or too small or that is for someday when you ____ (fill in the blank).

- Try to limit possessions if possible. If you have one item that can do the job of two different items, get rid of the other item. (Do you need a toaster oven and an air fryer? Or does the toaster oven have an air fryer setting that will work instead of having to keep both items?) Try to condense what you keep.

- Focus on what you need and what you use. Do you need four sets of bath towels? Probably not, unless you rarely do laundry. A towel or two for each person works perfectly. Try to get out of excess thinking and think *simplicity* in ownership.

- Do not let clutter have a place to accumulate. Remove any piles of papers or other cluttered areas in your home and replace them with something beautiful so things can't pile up. Find a home for everything, even where you put the mail each day, and make a commitment to clean up those places daily so nothing piles up again.

- Don't be afraid to downsize books. This was the last area I chose to declutter because it was the hardest for me. Keep only what you love and want to read again. Anything else can be checked out from a library or downloaded. Consider the joy you might be able to bring others (or even a library) by giving your extra books away so other people can read them.

- Come up with a cleaning plan. No one wants to spend a lot of time cleaning their home, but it still must be done to make it a healthy space. Come up with a simple plan, and then try to remember it as you declutter. If your goal is to be able to deep clean your home in two hours once a month, will you be able to do that with all the items you've chosen to keep? Don't let your material possessions control you or your home—take control over them.

Dara's Story: Downsizing to Live Simply

I grew up in a family that was the epitome of stability and the American Dream. My dad is a second-generation small business owner, and my parents still live in the two-story house my mom grew up in (with an attic and basement filled with heirlooms to prove it!). And yet, less than a year into marriage, my husband and I quit our jobs, gave away most of our earthly belongings, and started traveling full-time to serve in ministry. To the outside world, I'm sure it looked crazy!

But we had realized we would never truly be happy unless we were serving God with our whole lives. And all the things I had been chasing after were just distracting me from God's real purpose for my life. No amount of money, stability, or possessions could ever replace the peace and joy that I had found in Christ.

We've spent almost three years now living in a thirty-three-foot camper with our two toddler girls, traveling the United States to help churches and communities after disasters. We may not have a big house, lots of toys, or even a yard, but I have never been more content in my life. I love our little home on wheels, the simplicity of our family life, and the fulfillment of helping others. Our simplified life is all about being intentional with what we have so that we can be intentional about how we are living our lives. So often, minimalism and simplifying are thought of in terms of what you're giving up or giving away. But the peaceful life God is offering you in exchange for a few possessions far outweighs anything he is asking you to give up.

—Dara S., United States

It's Time to Start Owning Less

Ultimately, as you are cleaning out, decluttering, and minimizing your possessions, keep this verse in mind: "Take care, and be on your guard against all covetousness, for one's life does not consist in the abundance of his possessions" (Luke 12:15).

Do you believe that you are getting life from your possessions? Are you allowing them to define your life and the person you want to be? Or are you letting God define your life and who you are? We must be so careful not to get caught up in the things of this world. Satan is incredibly tricky, and he knows how bogging us down with the weight of our material possessions can keep us from doing the things God would have us do.

Clutter only adds to our busyness, and it simply does not need to. We don't need to be constantly rearranging our material possessions and tidying them up. There are more important things to do in life than cleaning and looking after our belongings. There will always be possessions we need to keep—items that are useful, that keep us warm and fed, that add beauty to our lives, and that we can use to care for others. But we just don't need to let all these worldly possessions take control of our day-to-day lives. As a wife and mother, I don't need to spend my days taking care of the inanimate objects in my home; I need to spend my days caring for the people in my home. They are what matter now and what will matter for the future.

five

Planning Simple, Healthy Meals

I remember the days when Pinterest wasn't a thing yet. When it came to figuring out what meals I would make for the week, I'd simply pull out my recipe binder and pick out our favorites.

When I attended my first conference as a blogger, I was introduced to Pinterest and asked many times, "Why aren't you using Pinterest yet?" I promised I would look into it after the conference, but though I decided I would use it as a blogger, I never got into it as an individual. Pinterest gives me anxiety, which is why I'm personally not a big fan of it. I look at all the amazing pictures, wonderful foods, fun activities, and beautiful DIY projects and think, *I'm never going to be that good at life. Do I need to be that good at life?*

But when I do that, I'm taking my value as a person and putting it up against all the beautiful, staged images I'm seeing and calling that "life." Is everything I'm seeing on Pinterest real life? Is my status as a mother determined by what I do or don't make from Pinterest? Are my children missing out on all those cute foods that look like penguins and dinosaurs and Santa hats?

When I think about cooking and baking for my family, my goal is to fill them up and keep them healthy. In a home full of food allergies and intolerances, healthy food is and always will be a priority for us. I don't need to feed them the prettiest foods. I don't need to feed them the trendiest foods. I don't even need to feed them snacks that look like penguins. What I need to feed them is food that they can eat, that we can afford, that they enjoy, and that keeps them healthy and gives them energy.

Perhaps you've gotten caught up in making the most recent popular and greatest recipes. Maybe part of you feels like your family might be missing out if you don't feed them the latest "Best Casserole EVER!!" that your friends have been repinning like crazy.

Many of us are prone to giving in to peer pressure when it comes to food and eating habits. This isn't to say that your friend doesn't have an amazing recipe to share with you or that you shouldn't continue to learn more about nutrition as new information is published. But when I look around me, I see so many people caught up in the best, latest, and greatest that it seems we've almost forgotten what food was put on this earth to do.

And God said, "Behold, I have given you every plant yielding seed that is on the face of all the earth, and every tree with seed in its fruit. You shall have them for food." (Gen. 1:29)

I'm sure most of us are aware that God gave us all the food we have to sustain us during our time here on earth, but are we glorifying Him with it?

First Corinthians 10:31 reads, "So, whether you eat or drink, or whatever you do, do all to the glory of God." Just take a moment and think about that. When you are eating that meal you cooked, are you doing it for the glory of God? Or are you doing it for the glory of man? Does eating a meal promote God's will for food (nourishment), or does it fulfill something else? Have we gotten so far away from simple meals that we've forgotten what food was originally made for? Has food really become a competition to be the best, just like everything else?

You likely came to this chapter thinking you were going to find my plan for simple meals and how we make them, serve them, and enjoy them (and you will!), but I also hope that this gets your mind turning when you are thinking about creating those meals for your family.

Do it for the glory of God, not for the glory of man.

Unfancy Foods

If you were ever to come to dinner at my house, you might call my family meals boring. We eat simple meals on rather basic plates, and there is always someone at the table who talks too much. But I love these meals. And as someone who eats three meals a day with all my family members, I'd better love them or they might get old pretty fast.

Just 58 percent of parents eat with their children on a daily basis, according to Pew Research.[1] I'm glad I'm one of the 58 percent. If I weren't, I would be missing out on so many conversations (the good *and* the bad) and on the happenings of our daily life.

When we sit down to a meal, it's no fancy four-course dinner. Breakfast is simple and usually involves eggs (thank you, chickens!), lunch consists of leftovers from the night before, and dinner . . . well, dinner is my favorite. I love the time our family has at dinner to talk about our day. I also love dinner because I just enjoy cooking, and dinner gives me a chance to share that joy with my family.

I can easily plan my meals without having to search through a mountain of cookbooks or surf Pinterest for hours. I know what we like. I know what is affordable to make. And I know what will keep them full and healthy.

I've been a meal planner for many, many years, but I finally feel like I've come up with a system that works well for us. On Saturday afternoons, I plan my meals and create my grocery list for the week, which takes about fifteen minutes. If I planned fancy foods for every meal, it would take more time to find the recipes, shop for ingredients I don't normally have, and prepare meals I'm unfamiliar with. I don't want my meal planning to take that much time because I have better ways to spend my day.

Here's a breakdown of how I plan our very unfancy meals for the week.

Breakfasts

I keep an ongoing list of breakfasts that my family loves. The list has no less than thirty different items on it at all times. That may sound like a lot, but keep in mind that these are all very unfancy things like scrambled eggs, simple French toast, and banana bread.

I love having this list in my recipe binder because when I'm planning breakfasts, I can simply go down the list and select seven items from it for my week. Easy and done within two minutes.

Lunches

Lunch is a rather boring meal in our household when we are home because we almost always have leftovers. Leftovers are easy for me to prepare—just heat and eat—and they don't take any extra ingredients or prepping. On the days when we are not at home or don't have leftovers, we eat things like sandwiches, soups, and salads.

I pair our lunches with whatever fresh fruit or veggies I have in my fridge that don't have to be cooked, such as baby carrots, cucumbers, grapes, oranges, or apples. Even if we only have leftovers, the fresh fruits and veggies liven the meal up a bit. Planning lunches takes no time since I don't really have to plan them; we just eat whatever we have in the fridge that day.

Suppers

Planning suppers takes a little more time, but not much. I keep a large recipe binder filled with all the recipes we've tried and enjoyed so much that we will eat them again. These are recipes I've copied from cookbooks, found on blogs, or gotten from a friend.

When I plan my suppers for the week, I select five recipes from my binder. I choose what I think sounds good for that week based on the weather (e.g., if it's hot outside, I won't plan on making roast beef, but instead I might make more salads) and what we already have in the fridge, freezer, or pantry. I then plan one day for eating up any leftovers. (I like to do this on Saturday or Sunday. We generally spend more time on projects or out of the home on those days, so I like to spend less time in the kitchen.) Then for the last day, I usually pick out a new recipe to try. If our week is going to be busier or more stressful than usual, I won't try any new recipes. Comfort food is best during those times.

Once I have all the recipes I need, I place them in the front of my recipe binder so I have easy access to them all week. No trying to find the recipe five minutes before I plan on making dinner; it's all right there waiting for me.

After I have planned the recipes for the week, I go through each of them and make a grocery list for anything I don't have. Lately I've been ordering my groceries for pickup to make this step even easier, and I do this right after I make my shopping list so everything is fresh in my mind. I simply find a store we can get to that week, create my cart based on only what I need, and submit my order to be picked up on the day we will be in town. Not only does this save me a lot of time by not having to go into the store, but it also saves us money since we aren't as prone to impulse purchases when we order online.

Here's one more thing to note about planning meals: I prefer to plan one week's worth of meals at a time in the summer but two weeks' worth at a time in the winter. This is because we have fresh food growing in the garden in the summer, and the selection at the grocery store and farmers market is always different from week to week. I like to be able to shop and cook seasonally, and I like to plan out my recipes this way. In the winter, less fresh produce is available, so it's easier for me to plan extra days' meals because they won't have as many different fresh fruits and veggies in them.

Sample Meal Plan

This is a sample of a one-week meal plan in our family, which will give you a better idea of how planning, list making, and shopping work together to save time and money.

Monday:
- Breakfast: egg muffins
- Lunch: leftovers and/or grilled ham sandwiches
- Supper: maple-glazed roast with carrots

Tuesday:
- Breakfast: sheet pancake
- Lunch: leftovers and quesadillas
- Supper: chicken, broccoli, and rice

Wednesday (a day out):
- Breakfast: breakfast cookies
- Lunch: sunflower seed–butter and jelly sandwiches
- Supper: slow-cooker chicken noodle soup

Thursday:
- Breakfast: banana bread
- Lunch: leftovers
- Supper: ranch chicken wings

Friday:
- Breakfast: breakfast burritos
- Lunch: leftovers and sausages
- Supper: cooked steak salad

Saturday (company for lunch):

- Breakfast: zucchini muffins
- Lunch: brisket sandwiches
- Supper: leftovers

Sunday:

- Breakfast: baked oatmeal
- Lunch: leftovers
- Supper: meat loaf

There are many ways that this simple menu can be made much simpler. For the particular week I shared above, I had already prepared all the breakfasts, and they were either in the freezer or in mix form in the pantry. I never pressure myself to do make-ahead or freezer meals, but if my week allows it, I do what I can to help make the meals even easier to put together during the week. Sometimes this just means chopping vegetables or washing fruit ahead of time that we plan on eating for snacks. It's a simple thing but it can help save time.

One thing to note about my menu is that I rarely plan side dishes, and I keep them simple, such as salads, roasted cauliflower, and fresh fruit, since I'm not always sure what fresh foods I will have in my fridge during the week. I could plan to make a fruit salad using grapes as a side dish for Thursday, but if my children eat up all the grapes for a snack by Tuesday, that would "ruin" my meal plan. I prefer to have a good list of side dish ideas and recipes in my mind and then prepare what I can on the day of the meal based on what's in the fridge. This saves us money as well. Often, I buy what's on sale that I know my family will eat. I don't run to the store to buy things at the last minute because I need something for a specific recipe. Using items I've grown in our garden and canned or frozen also helps to save us money and trips to the store.

Growing Your Own Food

One of my favorite things to do is to grow our own food.

No matter where we've lived, I've always had some kind of garden. I've had a typical garden, I've done container gardening outside our RV, and I've grown basic staples, such as herbs and greens, inside my house on my kitchen counter.

Growing 100 percent of your own food would be pretty difficult to try to do—not to mention really stressful and maybe not even possible, depending on the climate you live in. But I do think it's possible and very important to try to grow some of your own food. It's important to show our children where their food comes from, how much work it takes to grow it, and how we can rely on and support our community by buying the things we cannot grow ourselves. We can show our children that everything comes at a price, whether it be labor or money, and that growing and tending to food are gifts God has given us. I've also found that children enjoy learning about plants and nature by taking care of the plants in the garden.

This past summer, I taught my middle child what a tomato sucker is (basically, an unnecessary branch on the tomato plant), and he was fascinated by it. He carefully helped me prune the suckers from the tomatoes each week. One week, he decided to plant one of the suckers in the ground just to see what would happen to it. He was surprised when it actually survived and grew into its own little tomato plant. For the rest of the summer, whenever I pruned something from a plant, he tried to plant the pruned piece to see if it would grow. He didn't have luck with anything but the tomato, but he never stopped trying, and he learned so much about gardening, all from doing his own little experiments.

Considering all the different types of gardens, big and small, there is always a style of gardening that will work for your family. Gardening does not have to be expensive or complicated. It's a wonderful "slow" activity that you can enjoy by yourself or with your family. Here are some tips to help get you started.

Decide what you'd like to grow. Choose something that your family uses a lot and would really enjoy. Some foods that are simple to grow are lettuce, carrots, radishes, and green beans. If you have more space, summer squash and tomatoes are fairly easy and fun to grow as well.

Find out the best way to grow that food in your area. Can you grow it in the soil outdoors? What time of year is best to plant it in your zone? If you aren't sure, ask a friend who gardens. Most gardeners are happy to offer advice to someone just starting out, and it's best to get that advice from someone who already knows your area well. If you aren't sure who to ask, look for your local extension office or the master gardener program in your area. You should also be able to find some "gardening for beginners" books at your local library.

Plant the seeds together as a family. Don't worry about having perfectly straight rows of green beans or whether the kids put in way too many lettuce seeds. Green beans will grow whether or not they are in a straight row, and extra lettuce plants can always be thinned once they come up. My children love helping with planting. There is so much hope and promise when you put those tiny seeds in the ground and get ready to nurture them so they can in turn nurture you. My kids have been seen "tucking" the seeds into their soil beds, and I've even watched them sing to the little seeds as they helped put them into the ground. Planting something that they will one day eat seems like a very big deal to them, and they take it very seriously.

Tend the seedlings and the growing plants. Tending your garden doesn't need to take a lot of time. As long as you keep up with some general weeding (or use large amounts of mulch to help keep the weeds down) and water your plants on a regular basis, they should do just fine.

Harvest your bounty. The best part of gardening will come when you finally pick that big, juicy tomato and include it in your meal. Once the harvest begins, about six to eight weeks after you plant your garden, you may want to be in the garden each day finding what is ripe. Incorporate this bounty into your daily meals in simple or creative ways, or just do like my children and I do on many days—eat it raw as a snack before it makes it out of the garden gate.

Why Simple Meals?

Before my quest for simpler and slower living, I didn't think about what a big impact food and meals had on our lives. But when I thought about my goals regarding food (making sure my family is full and healthy), I discovered that I can do this by cooking things that are simple and easy.

There is nothing wrong with a complex recipe. Sometimes that's the only way you can bring out a certain flavor in a dish. But in our home, such meals are saved for very special occasions and are not the norm.

By making simple meals, we're taking the opportunity to enjoy the foods God has given us in a "nonfussy" way. Simple meals have also helped my children become less picky when it comes to eating, and they're learning to appreciate the food that is in front of them instead of craving greasy meals that are disguised with way too much cheese. Because of my own struggle with health issues, I want my children not only to know what types of foods they should put in their bodies but also to *enjoy* those foods. I hope that my making and serving meals this way will create healthy eating habits in them that they will carry into adulthood.

We've told our children many times that their bodies are temples, as stated in 1 Corinthians 6:19–20: "Do you not know that your bodies are temples of the Holy Spirit, who is in you, whom you have received from God? You are not your own; you were bought at a price. Therefore honor God with your bodies" (NIV).

There are many different ways we can honor God with our bodies, and we believe that one of those ways is by keeping our bodies as healthy as we possibly can. My husband and I teach our children that eating simple foods that are good for them is one important way to do this.

Of course, simple foods are not only a way we can take care of our temple but also a way to avoid the stresses that come with overpreparing a meal. You and I both know how much stress we have in our lives as it is. Why should we make things more complicated by making fancy, elaborate meals when we really need only to nourish our bodies and those of our family?

Lori's Story: Simple Cooking

For me, food and cooking have always been about love and making connections. It is an expression of love when we prepare food for others and when we sit down together to share food and talk about our day. As a graduate of the Culinary Institute of America, and as a food service professional for nearly twenty years, I have prepared my share of meals, ranging from simple to complex to multicourse meals, for a variety of audiences. However, none have proven to be as valuable as those prepared for my family.

Simple meals are ones that require few ingredients, utilize what's on hand, and typically involve uncomplicated, no-fuss preparation. In our home, meals are simple and frugal. They need to be. Our lives are busy, and we cannot afford to spend extra time on food preparation on a weeknight. We've learned that it's all about the pantry and the planning.

For starters, simple meals require well-stocked pantries and freezers. Throughout the growing season, my husband and I sow our garden with simple meals/menus in mind. As vegetables and herbs mature, we freeze, can, and dry them. We also keep our eyes out for special deals on pantry ingredients at the supermarket. Then, it's all about the planning. I plan from the pantry and the freezer.

I spend time each week planning meals—simple ones that not only pull from our pantry and freezer but also will last for the week and do not require a ton of effort to get them from the kitchen to the table. Typically, meals for the week begin with Sunday dinner. I incorporate and repurpose Sunday's dinner into other dinners during the week. A roasted chicken on Sunday will reappear as shredded chicken tacos, a hearty chicken soup, or perhaps a chicken pot pie.

We embrace the art of leftovers and look at them as opportunities for future meals. A pot of homemade meatballs and sausage in sauce will make several reappearances during the week. There isn't one complaint as the meatballs show up in sliders, a hearty baked ziti or spaghetti casserole, a wholesome soup with pasta and beans, or on Friday night when my husband prepares his sought-after pizza!

Pizza on Friday nights and a simmering pot of sauce on Sundays have led to our own traditions, like coming together as a family each night for dinner. Our children are open to trying a variety of foods. They occasionally participate in some of the meal preparation or cooking. Mealtimes are a place to share, a place to talk about things and ask questions, a place to reconnect. As our children grow, nightly dinners continue to provide an opportunity to slow down, if only for a brief time, to nourish our bodies with good, wholesome foods and take the time to reconnect. Planning, building, and keeping a well-stocked pantry make simple meals possible and provide us with the most sought-after ingredient—time as a family.

—Lori P. H., United States

Simple Meals Are Best

I hope this chapter has encouraged you to see that you don't need to make fancy five-star, five-course meals to keep your family full and healthy. You can save so much time and stress by just coming to terms with the fact that mealtime doesn't need to be a complicated affair and should be more about connecting.

Be sure to check out Appendix 1, where I share some of my family's favorite simple recipes. Not only will that section show you how to put into practice what I'm sharing in this chapter, but you might also find some yummy new recipes that your family will love.

six

Living Seasonally

Have you ever stopped to listen to the birds in the springtime? Have you sat down in the middle of a forest and listened to their songs as the warming spring wind gently blew the familiar smell of thawing earth around you? Have you opened your eyes to notice a purple crocus peeking up from the brown earth or a spotted fawn wobbling to keep up with its mother?

I'm often asked why we enjoy living in South Dakota and why we wouldn't want to move somewhere with less snow. While there are many reasons I love this place, one of them is that we get four seasons to enjoy each year. Living seasonally is important to our family.

The Bible often mentions seasons in both literal and metaphorical ways. God created the seasons at the beginning of time and said, "Let there be lights in the expanse of the heavens to separate the day from the night. And let them be for signs and for seasons, and for days and years" (Gen. 1:14). These seasons will continue while the earth is still in existence. "While the earth remains, seedtime and harvest, cold and heat, summer and winter, day and night, shall not cease" (Gen. 8:22).

As we read in Ecclesiastes 3, there is a time for everything. My family and I believe God created the seasons to provide a rhythm and a pattern in our lives. God is clearly a God of order and structure, so the fact that He created seasons to give structure to the year should be no surprise to us. We look at this as a blessing and take each season in stride as it comes upon us. Of course, there are midwinter days when we miss the summer sun, but if we believe that there is beauty and reason to be found all throughout the year, we can fully enjoy each season's riches while we are in it.

Eating Seasonally

In chapter 5, I gave a few tips about gardening and buying seasonal foods to complement your simple meals. In this chapter, I want to talk a bit more about how eating seasonally is not only good for our pocketbooks but also good for our bodies.

We live in a world where we can have fresh foods of all varieties year-round. Want strawberries in December? You can likely get them from your local grocery store, although you will pay a premium for them. And while it's fun to see some of that bright and colorful summertime food in the middle of winter, it always tends to be disappointing when it comes to flavor. Those strawberries may look and smell like summer, but they taste like cardboard.

Foods that are grown and enjoyed during their peak seasons will always have the best flavor and the best nutritional value. Foods grown out of season might have been grown far away and transported a long distance to get to your grocery store. They might have even been treated with a ripening agent to unnaturally cause them to become ripe. Studies have shown that this unnatural way of growing food and preparing it for the store is not beneficial to nutritional value.[1]

The foods that are currently in season and contain the best nutritional value will be based on where you are located. Our family's philosophy is to buy as seasonally as we can, use our stored frozen foods when we want something that is not in season, and remember most of all that it's completely okay to buy strawberries in the middle of winter if we really want to. While eating seasonally is a wonderful goal, it should never be an area in which you feel the need to strive for perfection.

When you are able to eat seasonally, take joy in what is currently available and make the most of it. In the spring and early summer, indulge in dishes that contain berries. In the winter, create homey comfort meals with foods such as winter squash. As far as cooking goes, take on each new season as a challenge, and discover simple new ways that you can prepare and serve those delicious seasonal foods.

Combating the Seasonal Lows

Do you have a favorite season? I'm guessing most of us do. There is always going to be something we enjoy doing more than other things, and if we can do that activity only in a certain season, we tend to gravitate most toward that season. This can create feelings of discord toward other seasons, and sometimes we may even spend months wishing for another time of year.

Please note that this is not to be confused with seasonal affective disorder, which has a different cause and can and should be treated with a doctor's help. What I'm referring to here is how we may find joy in one season but see only the negatives in another one.

If you struggle to see the positives in seasons besides your favorite one, I encourage you to keep reading this chapter. In the following sections, I will focus on some simple highlights of each season. Find things in each season that you know you will really love, and then look forward to those things each year. Appreciating the beauty in each season will help us to stop being negative about certain ones. Most of all, try to enjoy God's incredible creation with the changing of the seasons. Become a participant in the nature around you and immerse yourself in the patterns you find.

Consider birds, for example. At our home in the woods, we have a large population of birds that live here all year. In the spring and summer, we can enjoy watching the bright bluebirds and the hearty robins building their nests. We watch the mother-and-father teams raise two batches of babies, working together to protect and feed their screaming little ones. Then, in the fall and winter, everything changes and the jays arrive on the scene. These ornery scavengers try to find whatever food they can (including dog food). These large, beautiful birds don't seem to be afraid of us. They simply step away for a moment when we walk into an area they're in and then come back to continue their feast as soon as we leave.

I may not be able to enjoy the same types of birds year-round, but I can still enjoy birds throughout the year. We find it fun to observe how unique they are from each other: the different songs they sing, the ways they interact with each other, and the beautiful colors and varieties we see. God made everything so unique, and it's wonderful when we can rejoice in these differences.

Embracing Summer

Living in the moment during the summer season is quite easy to do, especially if you happen to live in a northern climate where summers are generally mild. For our family, summer is a time of planting and growing, fully immersing ourselves in the nature around us, and soaking in every drop of sunlight until the sun goes to bed late in the evening.

Summer also tends to be a busier time for us. With tending our gardens, preserving our bounty, and working on outside projects, there is always a plethora of things to do around our little homestead. We also take advantage of other fun summer activities in our area, such as swimming at the lake, going out for the day in our UTV, or hiking through the woods. Plus, we are big campers and will do some local camping in the summer (although we generally save our longer trips for spring and fall).

Even though summer can be the busiest of the seasons, it's important to find time for activities that will allow you to slow down and fully enjoy the beauty of the season you are in.

With each season, it is important to find a balance between productivity and simplicity. I believe it can be most difficult to do that in the summer, but summer also tends to have the most rewarding seasonal activities, such as gardening and enjoying the harvest or putting together a vacation and enjoying the family time.

Here is a list of fun summer pastimes:

Tend the garden.

Create new meals with fresh produce.

Learn how to forage for food in your area.

Swim in natural bodies of water.

Go fishing.

Have outdoor picnics for supper.

Have a water balloon fight or run through sprinklers as a family.

Go camping.

Make sandcastles at the beach.

Go hiking.

Take a road trip.

Have a backyard barbecue with the neighbors.

Take fresh flowers to those in nursing homes.

Visit the farmers market.

Embracing Fall

Our family loves fall because, for us, it is a time to appreciate all the garden work we did during the summer and to begin some preparations for winter. In South Dakota, fall can be very short, or occasionally we can enjoy mild temperatures through December. No matter how long fall lasts, it is filled with beautiful, mild days when animals begin to prepare for the long winter ahead.

During the fall, our family likes to travel and take advantage of the milder temperatures, especially if we visit any of the southern states. Fall is perfect for road trips and camping since it's not too hot, and most places we like to visit are still open for the year but generally less busy.

Fall is also a time to prepare for winter. Of course, this isn't usually something you have to do if you live in a climate where it doesn't get very cold or snow, but here in South Dakota, our winters are unpredictable. We happen to live in a place where we can easily get snowed in. This means a few extra prep jobs are added to our normal daily schedule during the fall. For example, we have to prepare our garden for winter. We also like to make sure that all the summer toys are cleaned up from the yard and that our pantry is well stocked with nonperishables. No need to panic or prepare at the last minute when the meteorologist gives the storm warning.

Fall is a wonderful time of year that reminds us that it's okay to start slowing down. As the earth prepares to go to sleep for the winter, we can also remember that it's okay to take a break once in a while and enjoy the colorful world around us.

Here are some ideas of fall activities you can do with your family:

Take bike rides.

Harvest and enjoy your garden bounty.

Preserve in-season produce.

Warm up on chilly days with hot apple cider.

Pick apples or other fruit at an orchard.

Bake pumpkin or banana bread together.

Plant bulbs for spring.

Create bird feeders and feed the birds.

Make or buy caramel apples.

Go for a drive to see the changing tree colors.

Embracing Winter

Depending on where you call home, winter may not be the easiest season to fully enjoy, but I believe there is much to be learned during this season. Where we live, we may be snowed in for days when a winter storm comes—a challenge I always try to accept with a joyful heart.

Being snowed in or just having fewer outdoor activities available means that life is forced to slow down. Have you ever gone outside during a gentle snow and stood quietly while the big snowflakes fall all around you? The earth is silent during those times when the soft snow begins to blanket the ground. It's one of my favorite times to just be still and listen outside because it's so peaceful.

I believe that winter is our permission slip to take a breather from the year's busier activities. For me, it's a time when I pull out some sewing projects, crochet new dishcloths, and fully enjoy the company of others. With all the holidays during the winter, it's typical for us to have extra company around. We also feel it's good to spend quality time with others not just during the holidays, and winter is the perfect time to do that. It's a time to reconnect and have fellowship with others in our home or in theirs.

While there are fewer activities to do outside in the winter, there are plenty of slower activities we can enjoy indoors during this time that we may not have a chance to do during the rest of the year. You and your family can embrace the slowness of this season with some of these activities:

Plan out landscaping or gardening for next year.

Go sledding or tubing.

Read longer novels.

Enjoy hot chocolate around a fire.

Bake breads or cookies as a family.

Make homemade kettle corn.

Write in a journal.

Make cinnamon rolls for breakfast.

Knit, crochet, or embroider.

Play board games.

Handwrite letters to friends and family.

Embracing Spring

Springtime is such a beautiful season of promise. The long winter is finally rolling back the covers, and the earth is waking up again after its nap. As wildlife begins to emerge from their winter homes, the colors and activities of the warmer months begin to appear again. It's a wonderful thing to observe.

Perhaps even more than winter, spring is quite unpredictable in South Dakota. We might have a beautiful seventy-degree day followed by twelve inches of wet spring snow the next day. For us, spring tends to be a mixture of summer and winter activities because we never know what it will bring.

Outside activities happen on the nice days, and we turn back to indoor activities on the not-so-nice days.

I believe spring is the perfect time to declutter and refresh your home. There is just something in the air during that season that makes me want to clear out clutter, create less upkeep, and prepare for the fun of summer without the housekeeping work weighing me down.

If you need some ideas for spring, you can review the lists for other seasons and skim the one here.

Plant a garden.

Have a tea party.

Declutter your home.

Visit a greenhouse.

Pick springtime wildflowers.

Go to the park.

Plant flowers around your home.

How to Live More Seasonally No Matter What Season It Is

Besides all the ways I've already mentioned that you can make the most of each season, there are plenty of additional ways to embrace all the seasons and live more in tune with their changes.

Get Outside Whenever Possible

It's hard to embrace each season and the changes it brings if you don't make yourself go outside. This is not an easy task for many people in the winter, but you don't need to go outside for the whole day; just a portion of each day will do. Perhaps it would be easier to find an outdoor activity that you like in every season and try to do that activity on a regular basis.

Personally, I like to go outside, take off my shoes (unless there is snow on the ground), and just sit and enjoy the sounds of nature for at least thirty minutes a day. Summer days are easy, and I may be outside from dawn until dusk, but it's still important to be outside during the winter, even for a short period of time. If you don't, it's easy to fall into the trap of feeling like each day is exactly the same.

If you can't be outside at your home, head to a park, local wildlife sanctuary, nature preserve, or something similar that will help you get outside.

Appreciate All of God's Creation

Often, we are so disconnected from the world outside our four walls that we fail to fully appreciate God's creation and the things He's made for us to enjoy. If you live in the city, it can be hard to find time or places to appreciate this beautiful creation.

Psalm 19:1 says, "The heavens declare the glory of God, and the sky above proclaims his handiwork." Are you taking the time to look at the handiwork of God and appreciate His thoughtfulness of all the details in things around us? When was the last time you saw the brilliant blue of a robin's egg in the spring? When have you taken time to view the marvel that is a dragonfly?

I believe that taking the time to fully see and appreciate these little things He has created builds up our admiration for our Creator. It's astonishing to think He created so many beautiful and intricate things for His glory and that we are lucky enough to be able to see them on a regular basis.

Embrace the Seasonal Changes Indoors

I'm not a decorator, but I do like to bring natural elements inside my home to embrace the seasons when I can. Please note, this is different from decorating for the holidays. Bringing in some of the things you find outdoors during a particular season and finding a way to make them fit into your home decor is a good way to appreciate the changing of the seasons.

This could be as simple as picking flowers from your garden in the summer and having a few vases full of them throughout your home. I can't seem to grow flowers, so we enjoy picking wildflowers and arranging them in a vase in the dining room. In the winter you could use some evergreen branches or even their logs to create a wintry decor. In the fall, you could make a banner out of colorful leaves and hang it around your living room. If you can't get some bits of nature from outside your door, look for these items at your local farmers market.

Get Excited about Weather Events

When we have a negative attitude about the weather changing, we teach our children to be discouraged by it too. Even though we know that not every day is going to be seventy degrees and sunny, we still tend to be negative about the weather when it gets in the way of our plans.

It's time to change this mindset by making the most of each day's weather, and this is really quite easy to do. If the weather is going to be rainy, think of some indoor activities that you and your family can do only when it's rainy. We like to pull out the card and board games or maybe get out some special toys that the kids don't normally play with. Rainy days are also great for getting in some extra reading time (either alone or out loud) that you might not always make time for. If you are expecting a snowstorm, make sure you have the ingredients for s'mores on hand. If you don't have a fireplace, you can assemble the s'more and put it in the microwave for about twenty seconds or until the marshmallow puffs up.

You don't need to do these special things every single time inclement weather happens, but don't do them rarely either. Create such a fun day that your children will actually rejoice when rain is in the forecast. This will not only help with any complaining that might happen about the weather, but it will also help them learn to adapt to any situation with a smile because there is always something good that can be found.

If you think you need to go out of your way to make what might be an unpleasant day better, you are wrong. Even something as simple as playing your family's favorite board game on a snowy day can brighten things up, and it takes zero prep time or planning.

Holly's Story: Joy in the Rainy Days

My daughter has always loved puddles. Or, as she called them when she was really little, "muddle puddles." We have a video of her, less than a year old, sitting in a cold spring puddle, covered in dirty water from head to toe. "Rock," she said, giggling with pure joy as she tossed rock after rock in the mud with a splash.

Whether it's saving worms stranded on a sidewalk or testing the laws of physics by sailing a wood-chip boat in rushing water after a storm, rainy days hold so much wonder and delight for children. A lot of adults, on the other hand, tend to feel irritated and inconvenienced by rain. If we have to go outside, many of us try to limit it to running to our car and then from our car to our destination. And going outside for fun in so-called bad weather? Forget it.

I remember once, when my daughter was a toddler, we were walking out of our apartment building with the express purpose of getting wet and muddy after a hard rain. We met one of our neighbors on the way out. "Be good for Mommy and stay dry," he said.

I understood where he was coming from. Cleaning up muddy kids, muddy clothes, and muddy floors is hard work. Still, I disagree with automatically equating the fun of getting wet and dirty with bad behavior. I think the benefits far outweigh the inconveniences.

Maybe I get it from my mom, who never got upset when we came home wet or dirty after playing outside. She said the dirtier we were, the more fun we must have had. The memories I have of playing outside, especially one particularly muddy day, definitely back her up on that.

The nine months our family lived in a temperate rain forest in southeast Alaska cemented my feelings about wet days. Every year, Sitka, Alaska, has an average of more than 230 rainy days and ninety inches or more of precipitation, only a little of which is snow. In Sitka, if you were to go outdoors only when it is sunny and clear, you'd rarely go out at all.

We quickly learned to do as the locals did. We put on our rain gear and hiked in the rain, explored the beach in the rain, and played on playgrounds in the rain. Fortunately, it was usually a light rain. I'll never forget our little friend Elias, a Sitka resident who found the rare sunny days unusual and definitely too bright for his taste. "It's not raining, Mom," he said. "That's too bad, Mom. That's too bad."

—Holly J., Minnesota

Living in the Moment

I'm so thankful that God created the seasons for us to enjoy and learn from. In our modern lifestyles, it's easy for us to complain about the seasons because we think they might hold us back from getting more accomplished or from doing the things we think we need to do.

But, like everything, God created the seasons for a reason, and I think one of those reasons is to remind us that things change all the time. Some changes are good, some changes are not so good, but if we learn to accept things for what they are and look on the bright side, we can appreciate the world around us much more, and we will become more adaptable to the circumstances in our lives. We can also teach our children this resilience and show them how to look for joy, even on the darkest of days.

seven

Creating a Useful Space

Do you remember when you first moved into your current home? I just know that you had big plans, didn't you?

That bathroom was going to be the perfect place to take a relaxing bubble bath. In your bedroom, you would have a neatly arranged assortment of throw pillows on your bed and a table on each side of it. And your kitchen would be a place where you would create delicious things for your family or friends.

Instead, toothpaste is smeared all over the bathroom vanity and mirror. Your bedroom has been a catchall, and you currently can't see the throw pillows beneath the pile of laundry. And your kitchen is so cluttered that you couldn't find the muffin tin if your life depended on making a fresh batch of muffins.

Take a deep breath . . . it's all going to be okay.

Even though none of our homes are going to be "Pinterest perfect" (because even the Pinterest-perfect homes look like that only for the second it takes to snap the picture!), we can still create a home that is a haven for our family and provides the useful spaces we really need.

I'm hoping that by now you've put into action some of the things you read about in the chapter on decluttering and minimizing. If not, I invite you to go back to chapter 4 and get started on that first. It's hard to create useful spaces in a home that is still very full of clutter.

In this chapter, we are going to do a deep dive into every room of your house. Once you've gotten it (mostly) free of clutter, you can start creating useful spaces that will help you live a simpler life and perhaps get your home closer to being that restful haven you imagined in the beginning.

The Kitchen

Our kitchen truly is the heart of our home, both geographically and metaphorically. I absolutely love having a bright, welcoming kitchen that I genuinely want to cook in.

Since our family eats three meals at home per day, you'd think our kitchen would be a stressful place full of chaos and mess. But thanks to the way I've set up and designed the space, meals are fun and enjoyable for me to cook. If you are not currently enjoying your kitchen, I hope some of these tips will help you.

When you worked on decluttering your kitchen, you likely cleared out many of the items you no longer use. Often in kitchens, I find appliances, cookware, and bakeware that get used only once every ten years or even not at all. We buy them with good intentions, but good intentions don't equal actions.

Maximize the appliances you have, and minimize the ones you keep. It's important to have a minimal number of things in your kitchen to help eliminate potential mess and disorganization as well as to simplify your cooking. If I'm in my pantry staring at a wall of appliances with which I could cook my meals, I might feel overwhelmed and confused about what I want to cook.

Instead, I prefer to have only a few appliances and baking pans in my kitchen that can do multiple jobs. I finally gave in to purchasing a pressure cooker a few years ago, but only because my slow cooker died and I wanted to use it for that as well. The cooker I purchased not only performs both of those functions but is also an air fryer. One appliance with many purposes! It takes up less space in my kitchen than three appliances would, which causes less clutter and fewer decisions about what to use to make a meal.

Make the space you have work for you. Even though your kitchen has a set layout, most kitchens contain plenty of empty spaces (cupboards and/or shelves) that allow you to customize your kitchen in a way that is most useful to you.

I personally prefer kitchen cupboards without any doors on them. I like to be able to see what I have and get to it with ease. You may choose to keep doors on your cabinets, but just know that removing them is an option that can potentially make your life easier. It only works well in a minimized kitchen though; otherwise the kitchen tends to look very cluttered.

If you are able to hang pots and pans, that may be another way to create a useful space. We don't often think of the ceiling as a good place to organize, but it can be! My kitchen ceiling is too tall to hang things from, but I have my three cast-iron skillets hanging on the wall right next to the oven. Easy to grab whenever I need them.

Stock pantry staples close at hand. Another way to make your kitchen a more useful space is to remember to keep your basic pantry staples close at hand. Even though I have a pantry in my kitchen, I like to keep all my spices and commonly used baking supplies (baking powder, flour, etc.) in a cupboard right in the kitchen so I can quickly grab what I need. This saves me time by not having to dig around in the pantry for a simple item. It also makes my life easier since I tend to buy many things in bulk, and I prefer not to have to lug out the bulk containers every time I want to bake or cook.

Store your dishes close to the sink or dishwasher. This will make putting them away very easy once you've washed them. We have a very minimal set of dishes (just enough plates and bowls for our family), and I keep them on a shelf right next to my sink.

Keep food storage containers near the fridge or the area of your kitchen where you tend to put away leftover food. Also, it helps to have containers that are all the same size, or at least all the same shape, so they can easily stack in your cupboard or fridge.

Set up a drink station. Depending on what you drink and what you drink it from, you may want to set up a "drink station." We have both an espresso maker and a Berkey water filter system in our home. The espresso maker has its home in the pantry, but I keep all the necessary cups, flavorings, and coffee nearby so they're easily accessible. Next to the water system is where I keep our glasses and the kids' water bottles so they are easy to get to whenever they need a drink of water.

Place items you use most often at eye level. In your pantry, be sure to keep things you use most often at a level where you can easily see and reach them. If you have extras of certain items, place them farther up (or down), and use them to replace the things at eye level when needed.

Maintain clean, uncluttered flat surfaces. Be sure to keep flat surfaces clean so they can be used at any time. It doesn't do much good to have a bunch of counter space if it's always covered in paper clutter. If you have trouble containing the clutter that accumulates on your kitchen countertops, buy some kind of basket to put those items in during the week. At the end of the week, clean out the basket, and put everything in its proper home.

By setting up simple systems and stations that revolve around the way you use your kitchen, you will find it to be a much more enjoyable space.

The Master Bedroom

I'm not sure why this happens, but the master bedroom in every house I've lived in has always become a catchall for the things we don't know what to do with. How many times has your child brought you something and you put it in your room with the intention of taking care of it later? Too many times to count? Yeah, I understand that completely!

But the master bedroom has the potential to be the restful haven you want it to be. With a little planning and organizing, you can create the space you were hoping it would be when you first moved in.

Plan a restful space. Take some time to think of a design that would make your master bedroom feel peaceful and like a place where you actually want to be. No matter how many systems you put in place, if you have bright neon-orange curtains thrown up on the windows in a quick attempt to block out the full moon, it's not going to be a restful place. (Unless, of course, you really like neon orange and find it relaxing.) I wanted a bedroom that was very light and airy (off-white with lace curtains) with some bright pops of color to make it a little lively. It really doesn't take much to create a beautiful bedroom, and a gallon of paint and some new curtains can go a long way.

Make the room comfortable. Do you have too many blankets or throw pillows on the bed to easily get in and out of it? Are there too many pictures on your walls, making you think of all the other things you need to do and people you need to serve rather than letting your mind relax? Is there too much furniture in the room? Are all the pieces really necessary to accomplish what you need the bedroom to accomplish (to be a place to rest and keep your personal belongings, like clothing)? Or are you keeping things in your bedroom that anyone in your home might need access to at any time?

Having lived as a family of five in less than four hundred square feet, I understand that sometimes we may have to utilize a space for more than what was originally intended. But I hope you will take this time to think about the things that are currently clogging up your restful space and consider whether they really need to be there. Is there another place in the house where they would be more useful?

Organize to meet your needs. Now it's time to think about the types of spaces you need to have in your bedroom. Do you need a place to get ready for the day? For me, this space is my dresser. I have my clothing in the drawers and all my hair and makeup items either in the drawers as well or on top of the dresser in front of the mirror for easy access. (I use this space for my daughter too so we don't hold up the bathroom!)

How close is your laundry area to where your clothing is? In designing our house, I chose to put our washer (we do not have a dryer) directly in the closet of our master bedroom. This makes it very easy for me to put away clothing. All the bedrooms in our house are upstairs, so I can easily put away the kids' clothing as well. In our case, it didn't make sense to have a main-floor laundry room because I don't have any laundry to do from the main floor! If you aren't able to change the location of your washer and dryer, consider other changes that might make your laundry routine easier for you, such as better positioning laundry baskets for collection or maybe a "family laundry put-away," where the family comes together for five minutes in the day to help put away the laundry.

If you have a nightstand next to your bed, use it to hold the things you need most while you are in bed. If you read at night before going to sleep, make that the place where you keep the book you are currently reading. If you knit or crochet before you go to bed, keep your craft supplies right there where you can easily find them and put them away.

Don't make life more difficult for yourself by keeping items far away from where you plan on using them.

The Kids' Rooms

As our children get older, I recognize more and more the importance of allowing them to have their own spaces and of tailoring those spaces to their needs.

Even if you have a small home and each child does not have their own bedroom (like in our house), you can still carve out individual spaces for each child. Even when our family lived in a camper, we all still had individual spaces to go to within our home, whether it was a bunk bed or a special corner.

Making your children's bedrooms into useful spaces cannot be done only by you; you will need to involve your child as well. Don't just ask them what they like to do there; observe how they tend to accomplish those things as well.

Make comfortable places for sleeping. The kids' rooms should be primarily designed for the same purpose as your room—as a restful place where the kids can get the sleep their bodies need. When you set up their bedrooms, focus on making their bed comfortable and inviting but not overly crowded with pillows or stuffed animals. (I know this is hard to do!) Keep all unnecessary lights and electronics away from the bed.

Assign an area for schoolwork. This area may or may not be in your child's room based on how they do their best work. If you set up a space in their room for this, make sure their desk has everything they need to do their schoolwork. You don't want them to sit down to work and be unable to find pencils, colored pencils, erasers, rulers, etc.

Establish areas to store clothing and get dressed. Do they need a space in their room to dress and get ready for the day? You can easily create stations just like I did in my master bedroom with a dresser and anything else they need to get ready.

Create space for play and creativity. If your child likes to do artwork, you can create an art station right in their room where they have all the supplies they need to create their next masterpiece. You could have a shelf nearby to hold supplies or a small storage container on their desk with drawers to hold all their creative materials.

Perhaps they love to read and like finding a cozy place to do it. You can create a cozy corner in their room with a comfy chair or bean bag right next to a bookshelf of all their favorite books. This should also be the space where they keep bookmarks or pens and paper to make lists of future books to read or just to jot down general creative thoughts that might come to mind while they're reading.

With regard to toys, we keep everything separated in clear plastic totes that are stored in the closets (no jumbled toy boxes). The rule in our home is to get out one box of toys at a time and clean it up before getting out another one. This has helped greatly with our children's independence in cleaning their own rooms because they aren't overwhelmed by toy clutter. Their closets are basically toy stations where they can easily find what they want on their own (thanks to the clear totes).

Let your children and their favorite hobbies dictate how you create useful spaces in their rooms. I'm sure your children will be more than happy to help you do this!

The Bathroom

The bathroom is probably one of the most used rooms in the house, but it tends to get the least amount of our attention when it comes to design and setting it up for function. Sure, you can likely do the most basic functions you need to do in a bathroom, but is its setup working well for your family?

Since bathrooms tend to be small spaces, you can't really have many stations in the room. It's important to think of what you really use the room for (besides the obvious) to make sure it's functioning at its full capacity.

Gather what you need in one place to start your day. Do you get ready for the day in the bathroom? Make sure you have a station set up either on the counter or in a cupboard in the bathroom to hold everything you need to get ready. This can be something as simple as a small tote from the dollar store filled with what you need, or it could be something as elaborate as several shelves to hold your things. Whatever you have the space for, keep all the "getting ready" things together in one place.

If you don't have space for this in your bathroom, you can do as I do and keep these things in your bedroom instead.

Store personal care items and necessities in or near the bathroom. Make sure you have space in your bathroom to store the things you use most in there. Items like towels, bubble bath, extra shampoo, toothpaste, and hand soap should be stored in the bathroom or as close to the bathroom as possible. Do you use the bathroom to fix bumps and bruises? Then this is where your first-aid kit and any other medical supplies need to be. Be sure to keep them in a locked cabinet, though, if you have any wandering little hands about!

Keep cleaning supplies nearby. Spit and toothpaste and other messy things happen in your bathroom, and it will be a much more useful space if you can keep it clean. I like to store a few cleaning rags and a bottle of cleaner under my bathroom sink (cleaning wipes, either homemade or store-bought, work great for this!) to give it a quick wipe down once a day and keep it looking and smelling fresh.

The Living Room

The living room of our home should be the place where our family can gather and enjoy each other's company as well as the company of others. It should be a relaxing, calming atmosphere that encourages connection with each other. Because of this, the living room should have adequate seating space, but it should also be easy to get around in. Take a look around your living room and do a quick assessment.

Assess your furniture, its arrangement, and its comfort. Is there too much furniture to get around easily? Is there too little furniture for people to sit in when they come over?

If you feel like you have just the right amount of furniture, assess how comfortable it is. Is it hard or overstuffed? Are there too many throw pillows to be able to sit down easily? Do the pieces of furniture face each other so conversation can flow? Or are they pointed at something else (e.g., the TV), possibly making conversation awkward? The ideal amount of furniture in your home will be up to you and your family and how you use your home. If you have a large family or entertain often, you will want more living room seating than if you have a small family or prefer to go out more.

When making decisions on furniture, don't feel like you need to go with what you think is "normal." When we arranged our living room, we found that a standard-sized couch looked too big, so we opted for several love seats and a bench. We still have plenty of seating, but it's easy to move around and doesn't overwhelm the room.

Determine what activities you do and what accommodations you need. Think about the things you generally do in your living room besides talking to your family and others. We like to play board and card games, so our living room features our "game chest," which is an antique chest I bought a long time ago and use to store all our games. Even if we play our games at the table, the conversation about which game to play seems to happen in the living room, so that is the best place for us to keep our games.

Does your family read in the living room? If so, this is the ideal place to put bookshelves filled with your family's favorite books. If the living room is where you read aloud together but not where you read individually, keep just the read-aloud books there, and put the other books elsewhere in your home if you have the space. You may also want to have a cozy blanket or two in the living room for snuggling while you read.

If your kids have some of their toys in the living room, create a station for those toys that will allow your children to easily clean them up when needed. A minimal number of toys and a small shelf work well for the living room. We've chosen to keep toys in the bedrooms for independent play so our time in the living room is directed toward family togetherness. (Plus, there's less to clean up in the living room!)

Keep flat surfaces cleared, and limit decorations. Try to keep furniture and shelving with flat surfaces to a minimum in the living room. If you have furniture like coffee tables or side tables in a living room, they tend to accumulate clutter very quickly. We've found that we don't have anything to store on those pieces of furniture anyway, so we don't have any of them in our living room. This leaves more room for seating and fewer messes to clean up.

Since we don't own a TV, we don't need much space for movies. We keep any we have (along with music CDs) in zippered CD binders on our bookshelf in the living room. I never found a need to store all the plastic cases for DVDs or CDs because they take up so much space.

We've found that the living room is the best place to display our family photos because they are always a conversation starter when someone comes to visit. I don't like to clutter up the walls with a large number of photos, so we stick with just the most recent ones. We've also stopped buying frames for our photos and simply print the photos on foam board and stick them on the walls with removable hanging strips. This makes it so easy for me to change up the pictures whenever I want to without having to buy new frames.

The Dining Room

The dining room is a very important room in our house because it's where we all gather together at least three times a day. For this reason, I want my dining room to be a place where my family (and guests) feel comfortable and not overwhelmed by what is in the room. When you set up your dining room, as with every other room, think of its main functions. Our dining room serves a dual purpose as a schoolroom and a place for eating.

Since my dining room is small, I have just two pieces of furniture in it: our table with benches and a Hoosier cabinet that holds extra dishes for guests and all our school supplies.

The big window in our dining room makes it very light, and we have a door that leads out to the deck so we can take our meals outside or go outside after a meal.

Store dishes and other items nearby. If you are unable to keep dishes next to the sink or dishwasher, the next best place to keep them is in the dining room, right where you will use them. This may be a good place to store your silverware and napkins as well. Use a cupboard or some kind of buffet table with storage to keep all these items on hand. You may also want to keep your salt and pepper in this area since you will probably use that at the table as well. If you have any table linens, such as place mats and tablecloths, they could be stored here too instead of in some faraway linen closet.

If your dining room is a multipurpose room, assign a place to keep supplies. If you work or homeschool from your dining room, be sure to keep everything you need for those tasks in that room so you don't have to carry notebooks or schoolbooks from different areas of the house when you need them. A small box of pens, colored pencils, erasers, and any other little items needed for school or work can be stored in the cupboard in this room as well.

Maintain a neat, uncluttered space. Keep the design of your dining room clean and open. No one wants to eat in a room that seems messy or is full of small trinkets covered in dust.

Try to keep your table clear unless you are eating on it. Allowing it to be a random drop-off point for papers or clutter will only frustrate you when you need to use it for a meal. At the very most, have a vase of fresh flowers on the middle of the table to showcase the cleanliness of the area and make it more inviting.

The Entryway

While not all homes are equipped with an entryway, here in the North, it's essential. We lovingly call our entryway "the mudroom" because that's exactly what it is for: to catch all the mud before it goes into the house.

When we built the mudroom, we built it with a very specific purpose, not to be something pretty that you see when you come in my front door (although it *is* what you see when you come in my front door). It's built for function, not to impress guests.

A mudroom or entryway has one specific purpose: to be the place where you put your shoes and hang your coat before you come in the house. Keep this in mind when you think about the stations in this room. It may be hard to think about this room in terms of its functionality first because we want to give guests a certain impression before they come any farther into our house. But try to put that aside for the time being while we address the functionality of the room first and foremost.

Create a space for each family member. Do you have a space in your entryway for coats? What about for snow pants? Mittens? Boots? If you use those things on a regular basis, this is where they need to go. In our mudroom, we have a cubby for each member of the family where they hang their coats and snow clothes and put their shoes. This helps eliminate the lost-shoe problem that tends to happen in most families with children. As long as we have a home for everything, it has a place to go when we are done with it.

Include areas for guests. Do you have frequent guests? If so, be sure to have a place for them to hang their outerwear as well. Something that's obvious right when they come in the door so they can easily find their jacket when they are ready to leave.

Provide storage for keys, bags, and snacks. The entryway is also the ideal place to keep your keys, purse, or anything else you need to grab right before you walk out the door. Set up a little basket for these types of things. (I also like to keep spare pairs of kids' socks here since we never seem to be able to remember to put those on before we walk out the door.)

If you need snacks to take in the car, keep some grab-and-go bags in the entryway as well. We have room for these in our pantry, so we keep them there, but we do keep some snacks for UPS and FedEx drivers in our entryway so we can quickly give them one when they visit.

Set up a catchall basket. If you find that your entryway tends to have a catchall spot for things like mail or other stuff that gets dropped when someone comes in the door, set up a basket for those things just like you did in the kitchen. At the end of the week, empty the basket and put everything back in its home, and none of the mail will get lost.

The Closets

A closet should be a space that works for you exactly the way you need it to. While each closet is very different based on how much storage it has, what room it is in, and what items you need to store in it, I still want to give some general tips on how to set up your closets so they will be functional and useful.

Store each person's clothing in their own room. If you store clothing in closets, try to store each person's clothing in the closet of their bedroom. This seems like common sense, but I know it doesn't always happen. If you buy clothes for future years for your children or store clothing for different seasons, try to store those clothing items in the bedroom of the person who will wear them and not in a random closet where the items may be hard to locate when you need them.

Provide clear storage totes for toys and other items. If you store toys in closets, try to store them in clear plastic totes. This will make the toys much easier to see and will help your children independently get what they want to play with. (You can also use clear storage totes in your bathroom for things like extra bathroom supplies or in your pantry for extra food items so you can see what's inside.) Anything not stored in a clear plastic tote should be in a clearly labeled container with the label facing toward you when you open the closet door.

Eliminate overstuffing. Do not overstuff any closet in your home. Overstuffing an area will make it a completely unusable space and will just frustrate you when you try to find things. If you feel like you have too much in your closets and it's hard to see what's inside, it's time to do a major declutter and remove anything you no longer need or use.

Paula's Story: Making It Work for Us

Many years ago, my mom said something to me that stuck: "When I was growing up, people didn't rush to fill a house. They couldn't. Furniture was made or passed down as gifts, a few helpful items were collected through the years and stored in a hope chest, and everything else was accumulated over the duration of a lifetime."

Fifteen years of marriage and several kids later, I have lived by those words, some years better than others. Instead of opting for a huge entertainment center, I repurposed an old dresser. The color wasn't perfect when I put it in the living room, but it could be painted later. The drawers hold everything we need, like DVDs and board games, and there's room for a picture or a few special items to sit on top. In our bedroom, we opted to move our dresser into the closet. It's very functional there and is less likely to accumulate random things on top. It also opens up our room and makes it feel less cluttered.

These choices have allowed us to live so much simpler. Less dusting, less clutter to clean, and we've saved a lot of money by being intentional about the items we purchase to go in our home. Stuff accumulates quickly, but taking time on a regular basis to evaluate if the things in your home still serve a purpose really goes a long way in helping keep the clutter to a minimum.

You don't need to rush to fill up your home with furniture and decor just because you can. Taking our time and being intentional about the items we have in our home has allowed us to create a very useful space for our family. We can have dance parties in the living room without being afraid of knocking something over. Our toys all have a place so they're easy to clean up. Our rooms are places of rest and retreat. My kitchen is organized, and every-thing has its place so that I can spend less time in the kitchen and more time outside with my kids. These are the things I want my kids to remember when they grow up, not an Instagram-worthy, picture-perfect home but a home full of life and love and giggles— lots of giggles.

—Paula R., North Carolina

Useful Spaces Are Happy Spaces

Once you've gone through all the rooms in your home, you can finally stop focusing on how you think things should be. You have made the spaces useful for you, and now you will begin to find that your life feels much more organized. Bonus: You didn't even have to hire a professional to do it!

Your home should be a haven, not only for your family but for anyone who enters through your door. By creating useful spaces and having a warm and welcoming atmosphere in your home, you've helped set the stage for communication, togetherness, hospitality, and fellowship.

eight

Creating Routines

Whether we realize it or not, we all go through life carrying out various daily and weekly patterns and routines. Sometimes they are made from careful planning and consideration, and sometimes they come from a lack of planning and end in chaos.

There's no doubt that good routines help us create a simple rhythm in our homes. This can be beneficial to everyone, especially when we are living in a fast-paced world where you never know what might happen next. Having a routine helps us focus on the things that do not change, things we can count on that bring us comfort and peace in this always-changing world. Routines also remind us of things we want or need to do.

Routines don't need to be complicated; they can be extremely simple and do not require much effort once you get into the swing of them. Our family has routines for large grocery shopping trips, for special one-on-one time between children and parents, and for the beginning of school days. We have routines in our home when it comes to mealtimes too, especially breakfast.

Having simple routines is a big part of slower living and can add a wonderful simplicity to our lives that we weren't expecting. This chapter will help you craft routines that fit into your family dynamic and might just help you create that atmosphere of peace and continuity that you are looking for in your home.

What a Routine Looks Like

To give you a better picture of what a routine looks like and what it can do for a family, here are a few of our family's simple routines. Of course, these are customized to our family's needs, but you might see something here that will inspire you as you create your own.

Wake-Up and Breakfast

Each morning, I get up between 5:00 and 5:30 (I let myself wake up naturally, so it varies with the day, depending on when I went to bed the night before). I have some time alone with God, and I occasionally have a small amount of time for my online work before I shower. Depending on what I'm making for breakfast that day, I take my shower either before or after I start breakfast. If I'm making something that has to bake, like muffins or bread, I will start my recipe at about 6:30 and then jump in the shower while it is baking. By the time I'm done getting ready for the day, breakfast is also ready.

The kids have alarm "lights" in their rooms. The alarm clock lights up green at 7:00 a.m., when it's okay for them to get up and come downstairs. (There are no loud alarms in case the kids decide they need to sleep in, which never happens in our house!) At 7:00, they head downstairs to breakfast.

During breakfast, our entire family sits at the table and eats together. This is when we talk about our plans for the day. If Mom or Dad is going to be working, we let the kids know. If we're going to town, we talk about what we will be doing. We talk at breakfast about anything that might be happening that day to give the kids an idea of what our schedule will be.

It's easy for us as adults to make a schedule and expect the kids to go along with it, but we've found that if we talk about it together, the kids feel more involved and like part of our family team versus feeling like they're viewing everything as a bystander.

After breakfast, the kids head back upstairs to dress and get ready for the day while I clean up from breakfast and tidy the kitchen.

It seems so simple, but that plan is like our morning blueprint. It helps us create a certain atmosphere that we want in our home right when we get up in the morning. Mornings when we stray from this routine tend to be more chaotic, and that does not set a good tone for the rest of the day.

Bedtime

We've been doing our bedtime routine since our boys were tiny. I think this is especially helpful for our kids, who have trouble knowing when to wind down for the day and who may have some anxieties about going to sleep, the dark, etc.

Since we get up early, our children go to bed early. After we have dinner in the evening, either my husband or I (whoever did not cook) do the dishes and the other parent helps the kids get in the shower. After the kids shower and put on their pj's, they come downstairs. We take a little bit of time to pick up the things we got out during the day, always making sure the floor is clean so we can turn on the robot vacuum cleaner. (Yes, I LOVE it!)

After we have tidied things up, we snuggle on the couch together, usually under one large blanket. We read a chapter of whatever book we are currently reading for school, and the kids also pick out several other picture books that they want to have read aloud. This is a special time of connection for our family, and the kids look forward to it every night. There's never been a night when they complained or did not want to read together. Some evenings, we read for a long time—especially when it's close to Christmas and we add in all our Christmas books and our advent reading.

When we finish reading, all the kids head upstairs again to brush their teeth. After this, our littlest one goes to bed. Then the older two can play quietly until it's their bedtime. They often choose to come back downstairs and read more books with Mom. When it's time for them to go to bed, they tell me good night, give hugs and kisses, and then go up to their bedroom with Dad to pray.

We love this routine, so our family has continued it for years. We've had to adjust bedtimes a little bit as the kids have gotten older and entered different stages of life, but it's been fairly easy since the main premise of the evening stays the same. The kids go to bed feeling connected, safe, and loved, and I think it helps them sleep better.

The other bonus of this routine is that it gives my husband and me a chance to be alone together for part of our day. If we allowed the kids to go to bed whenever they wanted to, we would lose that time together to talk about life and future plans or to just sit and relax in each other's company. Without this routine and strict bedtime for the kids, they might lose the sleep that their bodies need, and we might lose the time we need to build up our marriage.

Grocery Shopping

Since we live an hour and a half away from a decent grocery store and we aren't yet growing all our food, we have to plan a day in our week to get things from town. Typically I shop on Wednesdays, but sometimes I go out for errands on a different day or every other week.

The night before errand day, I set out the children's clothing so they are able to get dressed themselves before coming down for breakfast. Our routine on those mornings is similar to our usual routine. However, I prepare a breakfast that is easy to clean up, like muffins or bread, not French toast or eggs.

Next, I pack our lunch bag with our meal and snacks for the day. I keep a variety of ready-to-go items on hand for this specific occasion, and it helps save so much time and sanity! The bag, a large cooler, and anything else we'll need for the day goes out to the car.

Once everything is packed up, I go over my grocery list. I make this list on Saturdays when I go through my recipe binder and decide what to cook for the week. I also check sale ads for anything to add to our menu, but I can skip this step if I've already ordered my groceries online.

Before we leave, I make sure I know what we will have for supper that evening. We usually have leftovers from the day before. On the grocery days when we don't have leftovers, I put something in the pressure cooker, which I prepare the night before. This way we can slide right into our bedtime routine once we get back home for the day.

At last, I make sure that everyone is fully dressed for the weather and that I have my purse, my shopping list, and a list of where we need to go and what we need to do.

Having a routine planned around this day makes life much easier on the whole family and simplifies all we need to do that day instead of having to make it up as we go along.

Creating Routines That Work for Your Family

Your routines will depend on your family dynamic and the goals you have as a household. Here are some ideas of types of routines to help you figure out which ones might help you live a simpler life.

- morning
- breakfast
- morning chores
- one-on-one kids' time
- personal care
- grocery shopping
- before school
- after school
- meal prep
- bedtime
- tidying up
- midday
- laundry
- exercise / healthy living
- Bible reading / prayer
- fellowship
- cleaning
- gardening
- homeschooling

Routines are easy to create; it's following them and sticking with them that are the difficult parts. But if you start with a strong reason why you want to create one, you are more likely to succeed. Here are some tips for creating a routine.

Make a goal. What do you want to accomplish? In my examples in the last section, our goal for our breakfast routine was to create a slow, simple start to our day as well as to ensure that our children know about the day's plans right away. The goal of our evening routine is to help the kids feel safe and connected before they go to bed as well as to provide set-aside time in the day for my husband and me. Think about the goals you have for your family during the week.

Consider how to implement the goal. What time of day would benefit from a routine? Does the routine need to be a long one or a short one? What are all the things that need to happen during the routine in order to accomplish the goal? Plan routines around the times of day when they will be the most effective. If you are not an early bird, don't plan on starting a morning routine at 5:00 a.m. Make routines realistic based on what your days already look like. If you currently have no structure to your day, you will have to do a little more planning and a little more trial and error to see what will work for you.

Plan by the hour or part of the day, not by the minute. Trying to plan every minute of your day is almost a guaranteed recipe for failure. We have a few set times in our routines (breakfast is at 7:00, and current bedtimes have specific times), but I do not plan that at 5:30 we will do the supper dishes, at 5:45 we will do showers, at 6:00 we will begin reading, etc. Let the routine flow so it becomes a part of your everyday life, not something forced into place by a stopwatch.

Give it a go. Once you've made a plan, start it! Try your routine for a few days as you planned it. If something isn't working or isn't flowing well, make some adjustments and keep going. The longer you work at your routine, the more naturally it will become infused into your daily life until you realize you aren't thinking much about it anymore—it's just part of the daily flow.

Reevaluate routines every couple of months. Are they working? Are they serving their intended purpose? Does anything need to be added or adjusted—either permanently or for the current season?

What Happens If the Routine Goes Off Track

Some days just derail and go completely off track. By the time you get to the end of the day, you look back and think, *What a train wreck our day turned into!*

While routines can help keep our days on track and moving along smoothly, some things can happen that we can never plan for or expect. If your family has gotten used to doing a certain thing at a certain time during the day, it can feel like the whole day is out of place when something else happens. While we can't anticipate all the things that might come up during the day, we can plan ways to get back on track when something does happen.

If you have children, let them know when a change comes up. Sometimes this is the easiest way to fix things. Children are so much smarter than we give them credit for. They may not always understand why plans changed, but at least you've been up-front with them about it.

Make a point to explain which parts of your routine might be different that day. For example, if we have plans in the evening and come home later than normal, we don't skip the entire evening routine. Instead, I tell the kids we will only have time for one story that night instead of three. The routine can then move on with minor changes.

While skipping routines isn't usually advisable, sometimes it's unavoidable. If you have to skip one, don't stress about it. Explain to your kids what is happening instead of the usual routine and then move on with the rest of the day. If you are constantly thinking about how you "missed" a routine, the rest of your day will be thrown off. Acknowledge the missed routine and move on.

If you constantly find that you have disruptions in your routine, perhaps it's not the disruptions that are the problem but the routine itself. Take a look back over your routine for changes that can be made to make it fit better into your day. But keep in mind the goals you had in the beginning for that particular routine. If you find that a routine is not working well for you and you are always having issues with it, perhaps your routine is too detailed. It would be difficult, if not impossible, to make a routine that spans an entire day and be able to follow it precisely each day. Maybe your routine is too long or has too many components in it to be useful. Go back over your goal and then your routine to see how the goal can be accomplished in fewer steps or in less time.

Depending on the day of the week and your schedule, you may need to make adjustments to a routine. For example, we have one day of the week when we go to town and run our errands. That day has a different set of routines and plans than our other days of the week. However, since we are consistent with the plans for errand day, we still consider it a routine, even though that day is different from the rest.

Julie's Story: Helpful Routines

For our family, creating routines—or establishing consistency, as I call it—helps to create a sense of calming assurance. As a homeschooling family with younger children, we especially believe that establishing routines helps to keep the day running simpler and smoother. Obviously, there are times when this is impossible to accomplish. But we have found that if we operate on a schedule of sorts, everyone functions much better.

For us, this has meant a written note with chores or cleaning that needed to be done on a certain day or a written schedule of homeschooling work that needed to be accomplished. I believe that children look forward to knowing what needs to be done and that they find joy in "crossing it off" a list. It gives a sense of accomplishment for everyone.

You can also establish routines in the little areas. As a mom of four whose ages spread out over several grades, going to the library meant having a big selection of books, from picture books to chapter books. Our simple routine of having one "book bag" and crate, positioned in a certain place, meant we never lost a library book. There was a system, or routine, we followed that meant everything was accounted for and in the right place.

Creating routines, for our family, has been the cornerstone of each day running smoothly (for the most part). If you can try to establish just a few, they become simple habits that in turn lead to a more calm, controlled, routine day.

—Julie B., South Dakota

Routines in a Simple Life

I love routines because they help our family meet goals. They also help simplify our day and our plans. They keep us productive and the day moving forward.

When you write out a routine, it may not seem like it will help create a slower lifestyle. But when you actually live the routine, you will see how it really helps to create a nice, smooth flow to the day and allows you to meet the goals you have for your family.

If you are struggling in your daily life to find time to do the things you want to do or the things you know God is asking you to do, consider routines to help give structure and promise to your day.

Does the Bible talk about routines? Absolutely! Here are some examples to encourage you.

> She rises while it is yet night
>   and provides food for her household
>   and portions for her maidens. (Prov. 31:15)

When Daniel knew that the document had been signed, he went to his house where he had windows in his upper chamber open toward Jerusalem. He got down on his knees three times a day and prayed and gave thanks before his God, as he had done previously. (Dan. 6:10)

And he came to Nazareth, where he had been brought up. And as was his custom, he went to the synagogue on the Sabbath day, and he stood up to read. (Luke 4:16)

And Paul went in, as was his custom, and on three Sabbath days he reasoned with them from the Scriptures. (Acts 17:2)

While these examples don't give us a complete play-by-play of these routines, we can see that many people in the Bible had routines and structure in their lives, and they used that to their advantage to talk to God, talk about God, and take care of their households.

In the same way, we can use routines to create structure and harmony in our homes. We can use them to create time and space for things we want to have more time for, such as ministering to others, developing a better relationship with God, taking care of ourselves, and tending to the needs of our own families.

nine

Media and Technology

Although the word *media* has many denotations, here it refers to a means of mass communication that uses the internet, publishing, and broadcasting to get out messages. We use the technology of televisions, computers, and phones to access this media, which includes everything from our daily news about current events to social media to video gaming.

There seems to be a line drawn in the sand about accessing media. On one side, we have the camp that says, "No media ever!" and the other side says, "All the media you can get!"

I'm not sure how this argument has gotten so extreme in recent years, but I have a feeling it has something to do with control. One side believes that you are exercising control over your habits if you stay away from media completely. The other side believes that you can control yourself when it comes to media, so you are allowed to consume as much as you'd like.

My husband and I fall into a third category, one that I will call "Everything in moderation." Even in this category there is a spectrum of what "everything" means, and we personally tend to fall on the more conservative side of that spectrum.

Does that mean we will never own a game console and we don't have a TV? Yes, it does. Does it mean we will never access the internet or use social media? Of course not. In fact, our jobs are currently dependent on the internet.

Ultimately, whatever you choose when it comes to using various forms of media has to be right for your family, and it may take trial and error, along with praying for a clearer direction, to figure it out. Let's talk about media in general and in its various forms so you can try to make an informed, prayerful decision when it comes to this topic.

The Drawbacks of Media

We've all heard the argument "All media is bad for you!" but do we really know and understand why that is said? Here are a few reasons why letting too much media into our lives can lead to unsatisfactory results.

- Media can put pressure on us to do and buy things.
- Media can give us unrealistic expectations.
- Media can mislead us and falsify information, causing us to make decisions not based on facts.
- Media can cause addictions.
- Media can cause increased feelings of anxiety, depression, and loneliness.
- Media can cause us to become more self-absorbed.

- Media can cause us to become lazy and unmotivated.
- Media can give an easy outlet to dangerous things (such as violence and pornography).
- Media lowers attention spans, making it difficult to focus for long periods of time.[1]

It's important to make an informed decision for your family regarding media and to remember to use any form of media as a tool rather than as a life source or the source we draw our happiness from. There are benefits to using media (work, school, connection, etc.). These positives cannot be overlooked, but media should still be used in moderation for these purposes. Remember, there is no reason to completely cut out using media outlets (unless you want to), but you should still pray about your decisions when it comes to this subject.

The Bible says, "Your eye is the lamp of your body. When your eye is healthy, your whole body is full of light, but when it is bad, your body is full of darkness" (Luke 11:34). We need to make sure the things we set before our eyes are "light-giving" and not full of darkness.

Television Programs and Streaming Services

A study done in 2019 by the Bureau of Labor Statistics shows that men and women have an average of about five hours of leisure time per day. (Are you surprised? I was!) We spend an average of 2.8 hours of this leisure time watching television and/or streaming videos. That's more than half of our daily leisure time![2]

I'm a numbers person, so this is what that looks like:

- Average 19.6 hours (almost a full day) of watching media per week.
- Average 88.2 hours (almost four whole days) of watching media per month.
- Average 1,022 hours (more than forty-two whole days—more than a month!) of watching media per year.

This means if you watch the average amount of streaming media each day, you will have lost well over a month of your entire year to the TV or whatever device you watch on.

Do you want to spend a full month of your year watching television or streaming videos? Can you think of anything more important that you'd rather be doing? Does God want us to give up forty-two days a year watching television . . . even if we're watching good programs?

Our family has chosen not to have a television. Once you read these kinds of statistics, it's hard to imagine that all that time spent on one device would be worth it. This doesn't mean, however, that we don't still watch the occasional TV show. For a few months each year, we pay for a streaming service on my computer to watch *America's Got Talent* and *The Curse of Oak Island*. My kids even watch the occasional educational show (usually through YouTube and on my computer) when it fits into our school plans.

But we've chosen not to have our minds taken up by endless mindless programming. Although it's hard for my children to understand at the moment since they are young, we've made a decision in our household that there are much better uses of our time. And we watch the shows we do choose to watch only during the winter when we tend to have more leisure time or are stuck at home because of snow.

Do you know how much television you currently consume? Take a week and keep a record of your television watching (and don't cheat!). Record how many hours each member of the family watches (even when the TV is just on for "background noise"), and then tally everything up at the end of the week.

If you feel like the results are something you are okay with, you may not have any changes to make. If you feel uneasy about the time each of you is spending in front of the television, spend time in prayer. Psalm 101:3 says, "I will not set before my eyes anything that is worthless." Has our television activity become something unworthy of our time and attention? Ask God how He wants you to proceed with the television in your home and if there is somewhere He would rather have you spend your precious daily hours.

One of the most frequent emails I get is about how my readers just aren't finding the time to live the life they want to live. We need to take a hard look at our habits, where we are choosing to spend our time right now, to learn whether we can make more time for the things we really want to do. Habits, including TV watching, can be hard to break, but sometimes God asks us to do the hard things to live the life He wants us to live.

Social Media

Almost everyone uses one or more social media platforms, like Facebook, Pinterest, Reddit, Twitter, Instagram, and

Snapchat. In fact, 79 percent of Americans have a social media presence.[3]

That's a lot.

If asked, most people will say they have social media so they can stay connected with friends and family. But a study by Pew Research shows that when asked, people shared that social media made no difference in the closeness of their family in 44 percent of cases and no difference in closeness with friends in 49 percent of cases.[4]

Remember the list of media disadvantages I shared with you earlier in this chapter? Many of those issues stem from social media. Social media can lead to anxiety, depression, frustration, and bullying.[5] It is also very addicting. Social media addiction is known as a behavioral addiction, and it's estimated that 5–10 percent of Americans currently meet the criteria for this diagnosis.[6] Various acts on social media (getting likes, follows, etc.) light up the same parts of your brain as taking an addictive substance.[7]

When you think about it that way, it's a little scary, isn't it? I'm thankful to have grown up in a time where I knew life outside of the internet. But our children are growing up right now in this time. What does their future look like? If we as adults learn how to control our media and technology habits, then we will be more able to help our children, grandchildren, or others we have influence over deal with these things in their lives.

An important verse to remember when it comes to considering what role you want social media to play in your life is 1 Corinthians 6:12: "'All things are lawful for me,' but not all things are helpful. 'All things are lawful for me,' but I will not be dominated by anything."

Is social media helpful?

It can be sometimes.

Is social media dominating?

It can be sometimes.

Just as you monitored your viewing habits in the last section, monitor your social media habits too. Be honest when you are recording this, and don't be embarrassed by the results. This exercise isn't meant to condemn you but to open your eyes and give you encouragement to ask God if this is what He wants you to be doing with your life at this time.

Take a week and write down your social media habits and feelings. This will be a big task since many of us log on to social media accounts multiple times a day. Try to write down how much time you spend on social media, or at least keep a tally of how many times per day you check it. Record your feelings associated with your time on social media. Did a post make you feel angry? Did something give you anxiety? Keep a log of all this activity. If your children are old enough and are on social media, have them do this activity as well.

At the end of the week, assess your results. Do you feel okay with the number of times you checked in on your social media accounts? Or do you feel uneasy? What are some of the feelings social media evoked?

Pray over these results and ask God to show you how He wants social media to be part of your life. Social media can be a great tool to connect with and encourage others, but if you find that it has a negative impact on your life or is taking up too much of your precious time, it's time to reevaluate its place in your life.

As you work through this time of evaluation, also consider that how you use devices will affect how your children will use and view them. Though we have chosen to restrict gaming, media, social media, and television for our children, that does not mean they aren't still learning how to use a computer or how to look up information. We also aren't taking these things away and simply telling them they are "wrong." When the kids question our decisions about these types of media, we have conversations about why these things are not a large part of our lives. We talk to them about being healthy, about being creative, and about how there is so much more to life than what is on a screen. I may not have been parenting for very many years yet, but I do know that a flat-out "no" will only exacerbate the problem and make them crave it even more. Talking about why we do the things we do and why we believe the way we do has been much more effective.

News and Information

Forty years ago, the only ways to get news or information about topics of interest were to watch TV; listen to the radio; read newspapers, books, or magazines; or read documents, watch films, or listen to recordings in libraries and archives.

Today, along with those other technologies, we have the internet. Basically, the internet is a network that allows organizations, companies, governments, and individuals to communicate using "a mass of cables, computers, data centres, routers, servers, repeaters, satellites and wifi towers that allows digital information to travel around the world."[8] Through the internet, many of us get our news and information from websites, blogs, podcasts, streaming services, email, and newsletters.

Many people feel they need to keep up with the news and know what's going on in the world all the time. I am not one of those people. There are topics that I love to research, and I use the internet for that when necessary, but I feel no need to keep up with the news multiple times a day. It's easy for the news media to sensationalize topics because they want you to feel a certain way about a subject. Personally, I prefer to do my own research if there is something I want to learn more about.

Constantly keeping an eye on the news can give us feelings of anxiety. I don't know about you, but I don't have time for that. It's good to stay informed to an extent, but it's easy to fall into the trap of thinking you might be missing out on something important if you're not constantly checking the news. Plus, in general, most "news" is very discouraging and depressing. By subjecting ourselves to this type of content all the time, we may begin to have a very dim outlook on the world. Proverbs 17:22 warns us, "A joyful heart is good medicine, but a crushed spirit dries up the bones."

Are we allowing news media to crush our spirit and our outlook on life? Or are we striving to have a joyful heart? Can we truly show the world that we are a light in the darkness if we have the same dismal spirit as everyone else?

If you find that you are consuming too much news of current events, you can try a few different things:

• Limit your consumption to reading or watching the news once a day or less.

- Remove any email subscriptions that promise to bring you the latest news.
- Consider what type of news you find to be really important, and follow only that news.
- Try to use the internet only when you need to for research, and research only topics you are interested in.
- Designate a limited amount of time for online research—especially if you struggle with going down rabbit holes and bouncing from one website to another.
- Follow blogs and websites that have a positive outlook and do not discourage you.

Video Games

Video games can also take up a large portion of our day, with most consumers logging at least two to three hours of game play per sitting. These are large portions of our day spent doing unproductive and unhelpful things. But as I mentioned above, these things can be habitual, addictive, and hard cycles to break.

If you are a gamer, record your current gaming habits and learn how much time you are spending on this. Pray about your participation in this activity and whether this is how God wants you to be spending your time. I know that many people view gaming as a hobby, but as Christians, we cannot ignore verses such as 1 Corinthians 10:31: "So, whether you eat or drink, or whatever you do, do all to the glory of God." Is the amount of time we spend playing video games, or the content of the games themselves, glorifying to God?

You and Your Phone

Not to be outdone by our time spent on television, social media, and the internet is the time we spend daily on our phones. The average American spends just over five hours per day on their phone, with most of this time spent in less-than-thirty-second increments. This indicates that most of our smartphone usage is in quick bursts of checking in on various apps, and it shows that the use of our phones is more habitual than for a purpose.[9]

Should we allow ourselves to be continually distracted by the constant notifications and messages on our cell phones? Do we really need to answer those right away? If you find that you're too dependent on your phone, you can do what I did: Move to an area with no cell phone service so you have to rely on a corded landline to make all your calls. Just kidding. (But I really did do that, just not on purpose!) Seriously, if this is an issue that you struggle with, try putting your phone away in a drawer (or anyplace you will remember where it is!) for the day. Decide in advance when you are going to check it (I recommend around three times a day, during business hours, so you can return messages if needed), and stick to that schedule. Once you've broken the habit of checking in with your phone too often, you will start to see how wonderful it is not to have your day and plans interrupted by all the things that seemingly "need your attention right now!"

Self-Control in the Modern World

Being able to set limits is important when it comes to television streaming, social media, and other forms of media not only for ourselves but as an example to our children as well. If unlimited usage of TV streaming and social media were okay for me, my children would simply follow in my footsteps.

One participant in a Pew Research study about digital life said, "It has become an ever-present overhang on all aspects of life. There is no escape."[10] Media and technology have become completely overwhelming in the daily lives of many people. I remember when television screens were first installed at gas station pumps, apparently as another way to communicate with customers and show them more advertisements while pumping gas. Think about that for a minute . . . while pumping gas! Even in the mundane parts of our lives, we have to try hard to escape from the media that is being forced upon us.

It's okay to use media as a tool at appropriate times, but we need to exercise self-discipline so we will not be trapped in the time-consuming activity it has become. We also need to model this self-control to our children as they are being raised in this media-crazed world.

The Bible tells us, "For God gave us a spirit not of fear but of power and love and self-control" (2 Tim. 1:7). We don't need to fear this modern world; we need to exercise that powerful self-control that God has given us and teach our children to do the same. As they grow, they will have more media temptations than we currently have—probably more than we will ever be able to imagine—so teaching our children self-control when it comes to these distractions is the best thing we can do to prepare them for an unknown future.

ten

Family Togetherness, Hospitality, and Fellowship

Our country is aching for true fellowship.

Can you feel it?

Despite all our pretending that we are so connected to one another through social media, the truth is that about 46 percent of Americans say they sometimes or always feel alone.[1] The same study shows that people in the younger generations (millennials and Gen Zers) consider themselves to be even more lonely than those in the older generations. But why are we feeling that way when we live in a day and age in which we can be more connected than ever?

As my family started living slower, we found that something interesting happened. We finally had the time to connect more with others, practice better hospitality, and have more fellowship, but we discovered that others were much too busy for us, and we often felt like we were in one-sided relationships.

While I don't have a guaranteed solution to this problem, I do know one thing: If more of us start to live simpler, slower lives, we will all have more time for each other, so be sure to encourage your friends to go along on this journey with you. If they choose not to, don't be discouraged. Keep on being an example to those around you of what can happen to a person and a family who have decided to live against the grain. They are watching you, and you never know . . . they might just catch that bug too.

Family Togetherness

Since we started living a simpler life and changing how we do things and what we participate in, our family has had the unique opportunity to spend more time together than the average family.

And we actually like it.

Not all our days are perfect, and there are still plenty of sibling squabbles that go on in our home, but when I see how bonded my children are, not only to my husband and me but also to each other, I know that it's all worth it.

I understand that my children are most likely not going to have the easiest time growing up and going out into the world. Anyone who is raising children, especially multiracial or adopted children, will know exactly what I'm talking about. But I do know that no matter what is in their future, we've all been able to build a strong bond as a family, thanks to our family togetherness.

Family togetherness means fewer times going our separate ways and more times spent together. Instead of taking hikes individually, we go together as a family . . . no matter how long it takes the little one to complete the trail. We make a constant effort to do things together so we can grow in character together.

Alone times are important as well. My husband and I have alone time when we go to work or occasionally on a trip to the store when the kids can't be with us. Occasional date nights are also a good idea if you are able to get a sitter, but getting a sitter isn't something we are able to do on a regular basis. But, for married couples like us who are unable to have a regular sitter, it's still important to spend time as a couple. Because of our strong nighttime routines, we find time to be alone as a couple after the kids go to bed. Even though family togetherness is special and important, maintaining a strong marriage is also important and cannot be overlooked. When you are together more as a family, your children will notice everything more, especially your relationship with your spouse.

There are many reasons family togetherness is so important. Here are some that we've found.

Family togetherness builds communication. If our family is together more often, we have to be able to communicate our needs and wants to each other. By working on communication while our children are young, we are setting the stage for that strong communication to continue as they grow older, have more they need to share, and need someone they can trust and talk to.

Currently, in our home, we work on communication by letting our children know that we are always available to talk

143

if they need to. We tell them they are loved no matter what and that our home is a safe place to share their feelings. I'm always thankful for the times when our children come to us with their worries and concerns, even if staying up an extra hour talking to our child wasn't how we originally planned our day. It lets me know we are building that line of trust and communication that will be even more important in future years.

Family togetherness means kids are less likely to be involved in dangerous activities. According to one study, teens who frequently have dinner with their families tend to have better relationships with their parents. In turn, teens who have better relationships with their parents are less likely to use marijuana, alcohol, or tobacco.[2]

Family togetherness promotes healthy activities and healthy conversations. When children feel loved and know that their home is a safe place for them to share their feelings, they're more likely to communicate with their parents when things are bothering them and less likely to turn to dangerous outlets.

Family togetherness helps with friendships and character growth. Being able to get along with siblings and parents and learning to be a good communicator will help your children become great friends to others. By setting a good foundation of bonding capabilities and skills, your children will be more likely to use those skills to build good friendships. Family togetherness also can help facilitate character growth. With increased accountability by spending more time together and building those lines of communication and trust, each member of the family will be able to see their strengths and weaknesses and can help to build up each other's character.

Family togetherness builds your child's self-esteem. It's no surprise that having a strong family bond will build your children's self-esteem. Children who grow up in a home with this kind of bond are more likely to feel loved, safe, and secure. They will be more likely to use positive affirmations and feel confident in themselves and their place in this world when they know they have their family to back them up.

How to Encourage Family Togetherness

If your family doesn't do a lot together right now, the idea of increased family togetherness may feel overwhelming. You might even feel a bit smothered when you think about it. I hope you won't feel like this is something you *have* to do but rather like it is something you *want* for your family.

You can start by increasing your family meals together. Try to have supper together each night *and* try to encourage healthy conversations during that time (without any electronics!). For our family, breakfast is another important meal to have together. I make it special by actually making breakfast each day (even though the meals are simple, like scrambled eggs and bacon), and we all sit down together before we jump into the day. This is important for our family because it's our chance to meet before the day starts and go over our day together. Even though we may go our separate ways during the day, we are all on the same page and know what everyone is planning.

In the beginning, be intentional about the time you spend together. Plan fun family activities (miniature golfing, hiking, going to a museum, etc.), and also plan some ways that you can use your downtime together. Our family loves to read aloud and do puzzles together in the winter, and in the summer, we like to garden and take little nature walks around our property. Not all activities need to be spectacular and well planned out, but in the beginning, it may help to have a few things in mind to stop the "I'm bored!" exclamations.

Another thing you can do to increase family togetherness is to ramp up your communication. You can start small by just adding in more encouraging words to your children throughout the day. Then perhaps you could add in time with them: a special fifteen to twenty minutes a day alone with each child to talk about whatever is on their mind. For us, this special time has increased even more to an overnight stay once a year with each child somewhere away from home. This usually includes spending time doing something fun together (bowling, shopping, etc.), just the two of us, and then staying in a hotel where we can swim, talk, and bond one-on-one. Our kids look forward to that time so much that they talk about these overnights all year long!

However you choose to do it, working on family togetherness is never something you will regret. Many parents feel and know that raising our children is God's plan for our lives, and by creating an atmosphere of family togetherness and establishing an excellent foundation for our children, we are able to follow that plan.

Hospitality

Hospitality is the generous reception and treatment of guests (either those you know or strangers). Keep the word *generous* in mind as you read through the next few paragraphs.

Our family was recently told that we have a special gift for hospitality, but I doubt this is true. While it's true that we are givers and that we love to have people over to our home for playdates, meals, or game nights, I know we could be doing much more (and we hope to in the future).

The Bible has a lot to say about hospitality. Here are just a few verses on the topic:

> When you give a dinner or a banquet, do not invite your friends or your brothers or your relatives or rich neighbors, lest they also invite you in return and you be repaid. But when you give a feast, invite the poor, the crippled, the lame, the blind, and you will be blessed, because they cannot repay you. For you will be repaid at the resurrection of the just. (Luke 14:12–14)

> Contribute to the needs of the saints and seek to show hospitality. (Rom. 12:13)

> And having a reputation for good works: if she has brought up children, has shown hospitality, has washed the feet of the saints, has cared for the afflicted, and has devoted herself to every good work. (1 Tim. 5:10)

> Show hospitality to one another without grumbling. (1 Pet. 4:9)

The Bible tells us that it's important not only to show hospitality to other believers but also to show hospitality to those who cannot repay you. I've always felt a strong pull to help those in need. This form of hospitality has manifested itself in many different ways over the years (working with the humane society, fostering, serving at soup kitchens, etc.), but one way that has always been strongly on my heart is helping the homeless. While I would love to work in soup kitchens and food pantries again, it's not a feasible activity for our family while my children are young. Instead, at this time, we put together and hand out special bags for the homeless. The kids are able to help choose what goes into these bags (toothbrushes, deodorant, vitamins, dried foods, etc.), and they are able to help pack the bags too. When we're out doing errands, if we see someone who appears to be in need, we give them a bag. This gives us and our children a chance to see how this act of hospitality affects people in need.

While you may not feel like all acts of hospitality are do-able for your family if you have young children, be encouraged that there is still something you are able to do; it just may take a bit more creative thinking and planning.

I firmly believe that every family will find their hospitality "niche" if they are willing to look for it. Perhaps your family will work with the homeless. Maybe you will become a foster family. Or perhaps you will visit with elderly friends on a regular basis. There are countless ways that you can show hospitality as an individual and as a family, and these ways may change over time as your children grow and learn to show hospitality themselves.

Here are some things that we've either been able to do or are on our list to do while our children are still young.

- Make meals for those who are sick.
- Bake cookies for the elderly.

- Grow flowers and take them to residents in nursing homes.
- Pass out care packages to people in need.
- Buy and deliver groceries for those who can't afford them.
- Draw pictures and write notes and mail them to those who are lonely.

Kelly's Story: What Hospitality Looks Like to Our Family

I've never seen myself as a person with the gift of hospitality. As a young mom with four kids five years old and under, I struggled every time I stepped into another mom's home. Everything was put away. The lack of overflowing toy boxes left me wondering if their kids ever played. There were no Cheerios on the floor, and you could actually see out of the windows without a million fingerprints blocking the view. I usually left feeling like I must be some kind of failure, and I turned into a frazzled mess as I tried to keep up that other mom's perfectionism in my own home. My family struggled as I became shorter fused than ever with the natural mess that surrounded me. Finally, I decided I was done pretending. I started inviting moms over and left the mess. I knew I couldn't be the only one who struggled, and I was determined to never make another mom walk out feeling guilty for being someone they weren't. I was determined that this was hospitality. And for me, someone who isn't a natural Martha Stewart, it was. Being open and honest about my struggles is a way that I am hospitable, but let me tell you my latest lesson in hospitality.

149

I have a friend—let's call her Rita—who has one of the most beautiful homes I've ever stepped foot in. Rita clearly has much more money than we do, and with four children in tow, I could easily feel unwelcome if Rita showed even a hint of uptightness as she watched them disperse throughout her magazine-worthy home. Despite her beautiful house, I always leave feeling so very loved. It's as though every little detail was put in place to make me smile. A candle is lit in the bathroom ahead of time with the nice towels set out. The beautiful food is displayed with cute tags to describe the tantalizing flavors. The glass pitchers show off the cranberries and lemons that are playing bumper cars with the ice. Even the latte is made to my specifications. Rita has the gift of hospitality.

It's actually not about her having nice things at all. We've all been in that home where you feel like you can't relax as the hostess struggles to keep the tense smile plastered on her face. Rita has taught me that it's not the money or nice things that create a welcoming environment. It's the heart. She genuinely enjoys making a person feel loved and heard. One example of this is the way she gives gifts. She catches on to and remembers the slightest detail to give the most beautiful and thoughtful gift. Only once did I mention that a place an hour away sells the coffee I had fallen in love with on a recent trip across the world. Months later, in a thank-you gift for leading a group she is part of, there was a big bag of that coffee! I was utterly humbled that she remembered and took the time to buy something so personal. You see, hospitality extends beyond the home to a genuine care and heart for the other person. When a person really cares about you, it pours out of every smile and word and is one of the most magnetic things you'll ever experience. I feel welcome in Rita's immaculate home because I can tell that she genuinely wants me to enjoy my evening. I can tell she enjoyed preparing each detail for the night knowing how loved I would feel. The crazy thing is that I can be standing in the foyer at church and feel just as loved and cared for by her as I can sipping a delicious cup of coffee by her roaring fire. It just happens that Rita has a nice home and enjoys creating beautiful spaces, but Rita herself is who makes me feel welcomed and loved.

Hospitality comes in many forms and packages, but what makes it hospitality is that it is all about making the other person feel loved. If having an immaculate home and perfect food shifts the focus from your guest to your home and stresses you out so much that you can't enjoy fellowshiping with your guest, you've missed the point. My kids and I were once left out of a playdate at a friend's new home because she was very protective and stressed out about keeping her things new. Having five kids over was just too much of a risk. Life is short, and, as I learned soon after, you may not have this opportunity to fellowship ever again. A home doesn't last forever, but memories do. Don't let your stuff ruin friendships.

On the flip side, if not picking up the mess leaves you in a tizzy, unable to sit down and entertain, like a modern-day Martha, you've also missed the point. I remember one evening when our good friends sat at the table with my husband as I spent an hour cleaning the kitchen and washing dishes so I could relax. I still think back to that and feel ashamed at the message I was sending: A clean house is more important right now than you. How hurtful! It's a wonder they ever came back.

Whatever you do, keep the focus on your guest. If you enjoy having a nice home and adorable appetizers, don't apologize. Let your guest know you enjoyed preparing it for them and you hope they enjoy it. If you only have time for a quick cleanup and ordering pizza, don't apologize. Let them know you feel comfortable with them seeing real life at your house and that you're looking forward to catching up with them. Embrace your home and personality, then lean in and be attentive to your guests. Take the time to ask good questions and truly care about what they say. This is what hospitality is all about! It doesn't all look the same on the outside, but it feels the same on the inside.

—Kelly N., Ohio

True Fellowship

True fellowship is a wonderful thing that God has created for us. While the traditional way to view fellowship is as an act of simply being with one another or participating in the same activities together, I define true fellowship as something that happens just between believers. While biblical fellowship *could* include a meal or some kind of organized activity, it *should* also include prayer and support for our fellow Christians.

A note of warning before we dive into this section: Do not consider it fellowship and friendship if the relationship is one-sided. True fellowship involves caring for and encouraging each other in the same manner. If you cannot count on someone to be there when you need them most, consider your interaction with them an act of hospitality. The Bible says we are to guard our hearts (see Prov. 4:23), and we will quickly fall into a pattern of distrust if we try to trust our feelings in the hands of others who have no intention of being accountable. Although people make mistakes, it's best if our true fellowship is with those we can trust.

There are days when it feels like true fellowship and bonding and togetherness between people don't exist anymore.

We seem to be living in an age of self-sufficiency, and not in a good way. It's every man for himself.

We jump on social media and leave someone a birthday message and then pat ourselves on the back. *There we go. We connected. Good for us.* But is it really good for us? Is it good for those around us? Are we just taking the easy way out of things? I'm going to share a story with you that still hurts me a little bit, but I want to drive this "together but alone" point home to you.

When we were working on building our house, we set out to do the entire thing on our own. We could not afford contractors or hired workers. We had only cash to build our home, and we had a very limited budget. We desired to fund building our home with cash so we would be able to continue to live the simple life we were leading and so we could do as much ministry work as possible, which I'm sure you know pays very little. (Okay, okay, it pays nothing.)

I'm proud of all the work we put into making our shelter for our family. My husband and I worked at least fourteen-hour days for months on end to be able to get the house enclosed before winter. By October, it had already snowed several times, and since we could still see outside from the inside of the house (and I don't mean through the windows!), we were quite anxious to get the house done before another snowstorm.

Because of the delays in manufacturing during that year, it took four weeks to get our siding. Once we knew when it would arrive, both my husband and I posted on Facebook, asking our friends to help for just one day to put the siding up so we could have a safe and warm home for the winter.

Now, since we've lived in many different homes and have traveled quite a bit, we have many friends all over the US. We got a few comments on our posts from faraway friends saying they wished they could help, but local friends stayed silent.

Guess how many of those friends came to help with our house?

Not a single one.

I was so disheartened.

Where were all these friends who claimed to have our backs? Was that claim only good through a computer screen? We were blessed that my family (mom, dad, and brother) came to help us. It was an exceptional amount of work for so few people, and it took us a long time to get it all done, but thankfully God held off the snow again until we had most of the siding finished.

This experience taught me many lessons. First, it taught me that true fellowship and friendship with others is difficult to have over the internet. The internet and social media can be tools to help keep us connected, but they're not very personal ones. Furthermore, social media is often used as a crutch for those who want to have a false connection without any real action or feeling behind it.

In hindsight, we should have asked more people we have better personal relationships with to help us with the project, but at the time, we were both tired and a little desperate, and the thought didn't cross our minds. In some ways, I'm glad that God gave me this lesson to remind me of the importance of real connections and true fellowship. The Bible encourages these kinds of relationships, which we can read about in many different places, including the following verses:

> Therefore encourage one another and build one another up, just as you are doing. (1 Thess. 5:11)

And let us consider how to stir up one another to love and good works. (Heb. 10:24)

True fellowship is much more than just getting together and having a meal; it's a time for us to truly connect with other believers and encourage them in this life. When we slow down our lives, we are able to make time for true fellowship.

I always thought the adage "It takes a village to raise a child" sounded like an amazing dream. To have the support and encouragement of others to raise your family and get through this life . . . doesn't that sound wonderful? While it might not be possible for us to have the physical aspects of a village (raising families together in the same locality), we can still act on the idea of creating a village to surround our family while we walk this life.

Depending on how close your "village" is to you, this could look like caring for one another's children when needed. It could look like sending care packages randomly just to show someone you are there for them. It could be something as simple as taking a meal across town to a family who you know has had a long day.

I will warn you: Creating a village is going to take some work. Unfortunately, in our modern world, people are programmed to ultimately care for themselves above all others. But to have true fellowship and a true village mindset, we need to be willing to put aside some personal comforts for the good of those around us.

True fellowship is an amazing thing. It reminds us that we are not alone in this life and that there are like-minded people who walk this walk with us. It provides the encouragement and support we need to work through struggles in life and also someone to be there to rejoice with us in the joyous times. And it can help build up our relationship with Jesus, as we can study the Word together, pray for one another, and encourage each other's spiritual gifts.

So how do we work at having this true fellowship with others? Here are some ideas:

- Pray for one another.
- Share life together, even the seemingly boring, everyday things (small daily struggles, minor wins, etc.).
- Study the Bible together.
- Care for each other's children.
- Help each other when needed.
- Encourage and lift each other up in physical, emotional, and spiritual ways.
- Be a good listener.
- Share your table.
- Work together in a ministry or on a volunteer project.

True and genuine fellowship is something we all need. As the statistic I shared at the beginning of this chapter revealed, almost 50 percent of Americans sometimes or always feel alone. Do you believe we have the power to change that through our actions?

Perhaps if we just took the time to slow down from all the things that keep us occupied and busy, we could dive deep into family togetherness, genuine hospitality, and true fellowship. What kind of impact would that have on your family? What kind of impact would that have on your world?

eleven

Holidays, Events, and Parties

A few years ago, I hosted Thanksgiving for twenty people, and it was one of the least stressful holidays I've ever had. We planned ahead and didn't stress much about the planning, so we were able to relax and enjoy the meal and the day with everyone instead of being stuck in the kitchen. The reason that Thanksgiving was so easy on us and why we weren't in the kitchen all day was because we turned it into a potluck.

As the hosts, we made the main dish and provided the location for the gathering. Then everyone else who was invited brought a dish or two, and we had a wonderfully easy holiday meal. Potlucks are old-fashioned, right? I've heard that no one does them anymore and that they are tacky. Well, I do potlucks, and the one I'm sharing about here made our holiday a simpler and more joy-filled event because we could *all* actually enjoy the day.

To be the perfect homemaker, we have to be the "hostess with the mostest," right? We have to be able to throw the best party, complete with hand-dyed napkins, a perfect tablescape, and the best food people have ever tasted. Oh boy, I hope you don't think that's what I'm going to tell you in this chapter!

Think about why we celebrate holidays and why we host different events and parties. Is it because we want all the attention to be on us? Is it because life is all about the perfect appetizer? Maybe it's because our house is just so pretty and clean that we want to show it off.

Of course, it's none of those things.

We celebrate holidays because we are celebrating the meaning of the holiday. For Easter, we should be celebrating the resurrection of Jesus and all that means for us. During Christmas, our focus should be on Jesus's birth and how miraculous that was. Birthday parties should be a celebration of the life of the person who is having the birthday. Special events and parties should be to rejoice in a certain cause or meaning.

I'm not saying we can't throw a party for absolutely no reason. It could happen, but it doesn't very often. There is almost always a reason for a celebration, party, or get-together.

If the focus should be on the person, event, or thing being celebrated, then why have we gotten so confused along the way and decided that the party is all about what *we* make it? We put ourselves through countless hours of stress and planning, all for something that really does not need to be that complicated.

How to Take the Stress out of Planning

I have to be honest with you. I do not stress out about holidays and parties, whether I'm hosting them or not. There are so many things in this world more difficult than party planning that it seems rather silly to get so caught up in what is really just a fleeting moment when it comes to our timeline here on this earth.

That doesn't mean I don't plan any parties, and it doesn't even mean I don't sometimes get frustrated when it comes to planning an event. It just means that in light of eternity, small details really don't mean much to me, and I don't get overly emotionally involved in the planning process. I give myself permission to enjoy the day and the reason for the celebration.

I think my feelings are well summed up by Matthew 6:27, which says, "And which of you by being anxious can add a single hour to his span of life?"

Map It Out

If you are planning a larger event, don't do it at the last minute and hope that everything will fall into place. Start in advance to give yourself time and write out an outline of the event. Who needs to be in attendance? What kind of food does it make sense to serve? Where will this event be?

Answer any questions you have about the event and then look over your answers. How can you make those things easier on yourself? Can you buy some of the food premade? Do you really need to have that many people at this event?

Use this outline and your notes as your map to planning your larger party or event and refer back to them as often as needed.

Keep EVERYTHING Simple

Do you really need to send out formal invitations to your party? Or will a call or text do? Do you need to serve a full meal? Or could the party be hosted in the afternoon so you can just have snacks?

When you are considering having any kind of party or get-together, be sure to go over all the elements you are planning and decide if they are truly necessary in the context of what you are celebrating. Can you change any of those elements to make things simpler?

Consider Your Food Needs

Food seems to be one of the biggest stressors and expenses of most parties and get-togethers. When you are considering planning something, think carefully about the food. How much is really necessary for this event? Do you need to go overboard preparing fancy appetizers and snacks? (If so, why?) Can you ask people to bring food? What are some alternatives to making all the food yourself (e.g., potlucks, picnics, premade food, catering, etc.)?

For a long time, I did not make any special food for holidays. No, I'm not kidding. I was under the impression that if I did, it would mean spending most of my holiday in the kitchen trying to perfect a cut of meat or making the fanciest dessert. For the first few years of celebrating holidays as a family, I simply served our normal everyday foods because I wanted to completely focus on the meaning of the holiday and not be stuck in the kitchen.

This taught me some important things. First, that it's okay to make nice food for a holiday. There are plenty of foods we can make that become fun traditions at holiday times, like certain cookies or pumpkin pie. I also learned that I don't need to go overboard when I'm preparing these foods for my family. Now I take plenty of steps to ensure I'm not in the kitchen all day but that we still have yummy things to eat. I like to take steps to make the special day much easier, like making foods in advance and taking advantage of my slow cooker.

Downsize Your Party

We all hear of massive birthday parties that are held for kids these days. Perhaps you've been to one or maybe even thrown one yourself. Let me ask you this: Do you think the child had fun? Do you think they might have had the same amount of fun, or perhaps even more fun, with fewer people in attendance? Were those in attendance people the child wanted at their party? Or were they invited for appearances?

If you've been throwing large parties and they are not giving you the joy you hoped they would, it's time to downsize. We don't need to have parties that are overwhelming or stressful to plan simply because of their size. The next time you plan a party, consider inviting only people who really need to be invited, or simply skip the "extras" and keep it an immediate-family affair.

Party Alternatives

Simple party alternatives won't be your typical parties or events, but like many things in life, my family has found that the slower, simpler way of doing things can be so beautiful and rewarding. Remember, when planning a party or event, the focus should be on the person, holiday, event, or occasion, not the decor, theme, or food.

Intimate Gatherings

We often tend to go overboard with our party plans and end up with way too many people at our celebrations. That may work for something like a wedding, where there are many people you actually want to celebrate with. But if you are trying to plan an event to celebrate a different special occasion—a special announcement, a move, a new job, etc.—an intimate gathering might be a better option.

An intimate gathering is similar to a simple get-together with a small number of friends. You will likely sit down and have a meal together. No entertainment, fancy themes, or special rentals are usually needed. An intimate gathering is quite easy and won't take a lot of time to plan, but it can still be a very special event. Your guests will feel honored that you asked the few of them to this gathering, and they will be eager to celebrate the reason for the occasion. I find that an intimate gathering is much more of a blessing than a large event is.

Special Days

When our oldest child was younger, it was very easy for him to get overwhelmed. When I tried to attend parties with him, it never ended well, and we were always subject to the scornful eyes of others as the meltdowns ensued. I promised him that we wouldn't do that anymore. I understood that he preferred smaller, quieter settings, and I wanted to do what would make him the most comfortable, especially if we were celebrating his birthday. For birthdays, we stopped planning parties, and now we celebrate with "special days" instead.

On each person's birthday (kids and parents!), that person gets to plan out the day. They get to pick out what they want for breakfast, lunch, supper, their cake, and any snacks for the entire day. They also get to pick out one special thing they want to do. Some of the special things we've done include going bowling, fishing, to the pool, and to a museum. The meals we make during the day are for our family only, although on occasion we will share the cake with Grandma and Grandpa. Our kids plan their day months in advance.

These special days take a bit of advance prep. I need to know what kind of foods the person wants so I can get what we need from the grocery store, and I may need to make reservations or get tickets in advance, depending on the outing. Otherwise, our day flows like any other but with the birthday person feeling like the person of honor for the entire day.

Old-Fashioned Potlucks

As I mentioned earlier, I've read in various places that it's now considered tacky to have a potluck. But why? I've found that when you are having a get-together, most people want to help and will ask what they can help with. I always wonder if I'm being selfish as the host if I want to take all the credit for the party myself.

Personally, I love to give gifts and be helpful in any way I can. It's my love language! I'm always toting a gift along to someone else's home, even if it's just for an afternoon visit, because that's just who God made me. Giving to and helping others brings my heart joy, so it's something I always consider when I'm putting together a gathering. If a person is asking if they can help with something or bring something, are they doing it because that is their love language? Why should I deny them a chance to help? Because I don't want to seem "tacky"?

Potlucks can be lovely celebrations of everyone coming together and sharing the burden of work for a gathering. They aren't outdated, and we need to stop thinking we have to do everything ourselves. It's okay to rely on our community when we are together to celebrate a shared occasion.

Immediate-Family-Only Celebrations

There are times when we want to celebrate an occasion with friends, and then there are times when a celebration among immediate family only is perfect.

A good example is what I shared with you previously about our "special days." Those days are for our little family only, and they've become a unique family tradition because of that. Yes, we still enjoy gatherings with friends, but there are plenty of celebrations and holidays that are acceptable to celebrate with our immediate family only.

I also want you to remember that you are not required to have celebrations or parties with anyone outside your immediate family . . . ever. If you find that it adds simplicity to your life to hold all your celebrations and holidays with only the members of your household, you are completely allowed to do that. There is no law that states you must gather with anyone besides your family (or yourself, if that is the case) if you don't want to. Some people might be offended by your choosing not to attend a large celebration or party, but that is on them and not you. As long as you are able to give them a reason for your absence if they ask—and it's okay for that reason to be, "It was just too much for us to add that into our schedule this week"—that should be good enough for them. If we fall into the trap of saying yes to everyone and everything, we will definitely not be able to live a slower life or focus on what we really need to.

Small Ways to Make a Gathering Special

If you plan on throwing a small party instead of a big, fancy party, there are some little things you can do to add to this special occasion and make it even more unique. You don't need to overspend or go out of your way to do these things either. Here are some ideas:

- Create all the dishes or snacks together as a family.
- Let each family member tell you their favorite appetizer and make only those for your party.
- Have a treasure hunt.
- Have each person say something nice about the guest of honor.
- For holidays, read the Bible passages about why we celebrate that holiday.
- Get all dressed up, even if the gathering is at home.
- Do something out of the ordinary to make the meal feel special (serve sparkling apple juice, use place mats, burn candles at the table, etc.).
- Get creative at the dollar store. Let the kids pick out some party decor, and then be creative in how you use it around the home. We always hang streamers in the doorway that the birthday child gets to arrive through when they wake up.
- Decorate with fresh flowers.

- Tell stories with a theme during the event. For example, the stories could all be humorous, or they could all be about your favorite holiday. Tell your guests it's story time, and then tell them what to tell a story about.
- Roast marshmallows over an open fire.
- Go for a hike or a nature outing with your gathering.

Simple Holidays

Our family has a rather unique outlook on the holidays. While I grew up in a typical household that did all the holiday things (including Santa and the Easter Bunny), my husband grew up in a family that didn't celebrate holidays at all. That's right. No Christmas . . . nothing.

When my husband was finally freed from the bondage of the cult, we had a new challenge on our hands. With his newfound freedom in Christ and a strong desire to celebrate Jesus's birth and resurrection, we needed to figure out what the holidays were going to look like in our household since my husband had never celebrated the major Christian holidays before.

After much discussion, we both agreed that it was very important to us to celebrate the meaning behind the holiday as much as possible and that it was okay for us to have our own family traditions concerning the holiday season as well. The first time my husband celebrated Christmas was when our oldest was one year old. We were living in a camper at the time because we'd moved to get a fresh start after all we'd been through with leaving the cult. We hadn't established our plans or traditions at that point, but I will never forget that Christmas. We simply wanted to celebrate Jesus because we were both so utterly thankful for what He had done in our lives.

Since that Christmas, our focus has not been on Santa but rather on the Advent season. We have many little traditions we follow in December, all to prepare our hearts and minds for the big day of Christmas. We have a special Advent reading by candlelight every night. We make an extra effort to do more things together as a family (such as special baking). And we constantly remind our children why we do the things we do: why we have a tree, why we give each other gifts, why we give to others.

On each holiday, there is a special meal, but not one that requires me to be in the kitchen all day. I prepare ahead of time so I can spend the day with my family. Though we have our traditions with food and gifts and such, we always remember what the holiday is for and that our focus does not need to be on those external things but rather on the meaning for the season we are celebrating.

Keeping Christmas Simple

While other holidays can be busy, Christmas always seems to be the most hectic one. There are practical ways you can keep Christmas simpler in your home.

Set a budget. Shopping for gifts can be one of the most stressful things you do during the holiday season. But it doesn't need to be that way. First, set a Christmas budget and plan for it the year before. We have a small savings account in which we set aside money each month for all gifts (not just Christmas gifts), and everything we gift must come out of that budget.

Make a list of what to get. When it gets close to Christmastime, we make a list of the people we need to shop for and what we would like to get them. We have a set budget per person and can't go over this amount.

Make an agreement about gifts. We have made decisions about how much gifting we do within our family. Our extended family does a gift exchange among the adults, so each adult has to buy for only one other adult, and we do small gifts for the kids. Within our household, we have always bought just three presents per child and only a handful of stocking gifts. There isn't a particular reason for this number except that it seemed like a good number of gifts when we tried it out. Enough to get them what they need, but not so much that it's too much. This year, however, we've decided to cut out all material gifts and start doing experience gifts only. This was a decision we made with our children, and even though they are young, they are excited to help us decide what special thing we will do for Christmas.

By having a list and a budget (and sticking to them!), we've made the gift shopping much easier on ourselves, and it's something I stress very little over each year. We aren't buying in excess just for the sake of buying gifts.

Plan one baking day. Baking is so much fun during Christmastime because we tend to make all the yummy things we don't make during the rest of the year. But it's easy to get overwhelmed with all the baking you want to do.

If you have a lot of food that you are planning to make, you might want to plan a big baking day instead of just making one or two things each day. Make room in your freezer, and freeze the things you don't need right away for later. One big baking day and you are done!

Have a cookie exchange. Just because you want to have twelve different kinds of cookies doesn't mean you need to make them all. Invite several of your friends or family members to participate in a cookie exchange, and have each participant make a dozen cookies. (Make sure you are each making a different kind!) Then get together and exchange your cookies so you all end up with several different kinds.

Buy goodies from a bakery. If you don't want treats this Christmas or if you are perfectly happy with what the local bakery has to offer, just don't bake. Take a year off. You want your holiday to be simple, and if baking is going to stress you out, then come up with an alternative. We all know we are going to fill up on plenty of goodies during holiday parties anyway.

Set extra time for fellowship. Yes, we all see family during the holidays and maybe even exchange gifts, but it may be difficult to get one-on-one time with each other in that setting. Take time to invite a family member for lunch or have your cousins over for a small impromptu dinner. Take the littles in your family to a local event. Make Christmas Eve a family game night.

Whatever you end up doing, take time to appreciate being together with one another in some way.

Donate and be generous. Although anytime is a wonderful time to think of others, most of us feel particularly generous during the Christmas season. There are many ways to take advantage of those feelings of goodwill toward others.

Do we really appreciate all the special baked goodies we make or receive? Do we appreciate our huge Christmas feasts? Offer your excess to a family in need or take time during the holiday season to work for a day at a soup kitchen.

You can also grab some extras at the grocery store during all the great holiday sales and donate them to your local food pantry. It's a very simple way to remind our children that this is a time to think about others, not just ourselves and what we want during Christmas.

Another nice idea is to take treats to a local senior center or to seniors' homes. They love the goodies, and they are often forgotten.

Christmas is also a time of excess clutter in our homes. Every year after Christmas, we take the time to go through our kids' things with them to find everything they've outgrown and no longer play with. We donate all these items to places where someone else will be able to enjoy them.

Beth's Story: Simple Celebrations

I am a planner and a perfectionist—I love putting together all the details of the perfect event, from the decorations to the food. When my oldest daughter was born, I relished the idea of putting together perfectly themed birthday parties, and I scoured Pinterest for ideas. For her first birthday, we had a ladybug-themed party inspired by her favorite toy—a stuffed animal ladybug that we couldn't leave home without! I bought her a ladybug outfit, we printed ladybug invitations, and we had ladybug decorations and food. This concept continued after my second and third daughters were born, but it got more and more difficult to come up with the perfect theme, and it got expensive buying everything three times a year!

As they got into school, the parties grew larger because they wanted to invite school friends. I found myself so stressed, I wasn't finding my usual joy in the planning process. And while I was creating the perfect party for pictures, in reality, I wasn't enjoying any aspect of the party itself. Even worse, I was missing the whole point—celebrating the births of my daughters! I finally let go of my ridiculous standards, and we started inviting only immediate family and maybe a close friend or two. Since all their birthdays are during the spring/summer, my husband would grill hamburgers and hot dogs to take the stress of food prep off me. We kept decorations minimal—themed paper goods and a cake.

I put my camera down and was finally able to enjoy celebrating the beautiful daughters God had given me!

When it came to Christmas, it was no different. Growing up, we didn't celebrate Christmas—no lights, no tree, no gifts. When I had my own family, I was excited about being able to create the holiday traditions I never had. I wanted to do *all* the things—have the perfectly decorated tree, go see all the Christmas light displays, bake the perfect Christmas cookies, have perfectly wrapped presents, and cook the best Christmas dinner. Once again, I was letting the stress of trying to fit everything in and get it just right rob me of the joy of the season.

A friend of mine posted a quote on Facebook that changed my entire perspective: "You are not responsible for making this time of year special or magical for everyone around you. Jesus already did that." How convincing! And how refreshing it was to focus on the real meaning of the season! We started celebrating with just the five of us. Instead of buying lots of toys our kids didn't need, we focused on "experiences"—dance or art classes and tickets to local attractions. Rather than decorating the tree and cookies myself so they would look just right, I had the kids help me. We read an Advent storybook and attended Christmas Eve service together.

Creating these events and traditions is still important to me, but now, instead of centering on being "perfect," my focus is on Jesus and the five of us in our family—truly the most important things!

—Beth F., Kansas

Stop the Stress

With so many ways to keep holidays, parties, and special events simple and relaxed, I hope you will stop feeling the burden of stress that you might have previously felt when it came to these things.

Ultimately, we need to remember the reasons we are celebrating during these times and keep in mind what the person wants or what the meaning of the holiday is—not our own selfish desires about how things should be.

You might be concerned that people will have expectations of how you should do things: how you should throw a party, how you should celebrate a certain holiday. But they don't get to decide how you do things; only you do.

twelve

You Have Permission to Slow Down

Friend, are you tired? Does the busyness of everyday life leave you exhausted and just wanting to lay your head down at the end of the day to try to get some rest before you have to get up and do it all over again? Is that rest even restful? Or do vivid dreams of what you still need to accomplish run through your mind while you are sleeping?

Many days when I'm working on something I enjoy—caring for my garden, watching the kids play in the yard, or just sitting down writing—I think about the girl I was not so long ago. The one who tried to do it all so we could have it all. The one who was so tired after lunch that I had to nap when the kids napped. While we still have busy days (and always will), I'm so incredibly thankful that I finally gave myself permission to slow things down.

Review these questions and answer honestly:

- Why do we believe every moment in our life must be productive?
- Why does the thought of slowing down scare us?
- Why do we feel the need to justify our existence by being constantly busy?
- Why do we think we aren't allowed to rest?

You may not realize outright that you aren't giving yourself permission to rest or slow down, but I bet that deep down in your subconscious you are thinking these things.

According to the American Institute of Stress, "it has been estimated that 75–90 percent of all visits to primary care physicians are for stress related problems."[1]

Did you read that? More often than not, a visit to a general doctor in the United States is for *stress*. I think we have a little more than a struggle on our hands; we have an epidemic of worry and busyness that is affecting not only our day-to-day lives but our health as well.

But why is it that we are so busy all the time? Do we really have that much we need to get done?

Reasons Why We Are Busy

Procrastination

The book of Proverbs has quite a bit to say about the topics of laziness and procrastination. Verses like Proverbs 10:4, which says, "A slack hand causes poverty, but the hand of the diligent makes rich," are reminders to us that there is no reason to put things off that we need to get done. We all have things we don't really want to do, but by putting them off day after day, they begin to pile up, and we become overwhelmed and incredibly busy trying to catch up with everything.

If we can learn to be diligent about our time and accomplish the tasks we need to do when we need to do them, we won't have to worry about feeling overwhelmed anymore.

Avoiding Our Thoughts

Our thoughts and feelings can often provoke anxiety, fear, worry, and other uncomfortable stress reactions and emotions. These thoughts and feelings may come from problems in our life that we want to avoid dealing with. We might feel lonely, unworthy, bored, like we are missing out on something, or like life is passing us by. It's often easier to cover up these thoughts than to deal with them. So, instead of dealing with these feelings or issues, or simply renewing the thoughts in our mind by praying and reading Scripture, we often choose to fill our time with unnecessary busyness.

This is something we all do. One day, while I was coming to the end of writing this book, I told my husband I needed to get out and be busy all day because the chapter I was writing was stressing me out. He asked me, "What's the chapter about?" I answered, feeling like a complete hypocrite, "It's about procrastination, avoidance, and guilt."

Like I said, we all do this from time to time. We all have difficult things in life that we don't really want to deal with. Instead of trying to cover up those feelings with extra busywork, we need to learn how to deal with them in a mature, Christian way. We need to stop, we need to pray, and we need to search Scripture to see if God has given us an answer

175

for the situation. Those feelings will never fully be covered up by all that busyness because you know that by the time you run out of things to do, the thought or issue will still need to be dealt with. All you do by putting it off is make things worse.

Culture

We live in a culture where it is completely acceptable to be busy all the time. Not only is it acceptable, but it's also commendable.

"How have you been lately?"

"Oh, we've been keeping so busy!"

Have you ever said that before? I have. We live in a world that has coined the phrase *twenty-four seven*, and we feel like each of those twenty-four hours a day, seven days a week must be filled with productivity. Any rest or downtime might be considered laziness, and we definitely don't want to be labeled "lazy."

Many of us inherited this idea from our families. My ancestors were German and Bohemian pioneers who had to carve out a life for their families on the very difficult plains of the Dakota Territory. They had to work hard or they would have died from a number of things, including sickness, starvation, farm accidents, and more. That spirit of hard work has been passed down from generation to generation in our family, and when you come from something like that, it's hard to get in the mindset that a little rest is okay.

There is also the message that is passed around in our American culture that if you aren't productive, you might be useless. Not worth anything. Messy. Have you bought into that lie?

Saying Yes

Raise your hand if you are a people pleaser. You can't see me, but I've raised both hands. For some of us, the inability to say no causes many issues and unnecessary busyness. How hard is it to take on just one more task? Or add one more thing to your job? Or let the kids be in one more activity?

It's so easy to add things to your plate, one at a time, without realizing that all those things pile up. Eventually you reach a breaking point when you have more things than you can possibly accomplish, all because you couldn't say no.

We have to learn to be more generous with our *no*s so we can be more generous with our *yes*es. After all, if you've taken on more than you can handle and are now busy for the rest of the month, how are you going to say yes when that opportunity comes along to do a last-minute service project with your family? Or how will you snatch up that amazing deal on a weekend cabin getaway with your spouse for some seriously needed one-on-one time?

We are often too quick to give an answer when we need to remember to think it over first. There is nothing wrong with telling someone, "Let me think about it" or "Let me pray about it" before you give them an answer. If you are too quick to say yes, you will probably become the person they come to for all the things they need someone else to do. That's a good way for you to quickly get overwhelmed and feel used.

Guilt

Even as a people pleaser, I'm not sure I really understood what guilt was until I was a mom. The Bible tells us to cast all our anxieties on God because He cares for us (1 Pet. 5:7).

When we feel guilt start to creep in—the guilt of not letting our kids do certain things, the guilt of our home not being a certain way, the guilt of not feeling like we are enough—are we casting our anxiety on Him? Or are we creating more busyness for ourselves so we don't have to deal with the guilt feelings anymore?

We need to stop covering things up with busyness. We need to allow ourselves to be who God really wants us to be, and we need to be brave enough to ask Him how we need to handle things. It seems we so often forget that we aren't doing this alone; God is on our team.

Productivity and Idolatry

Idolatry is what happens when something takes the place of God in our lives. It can happen with many different things: our spouse, our children, our job. Anything can become an idol, including productivity. As Christians, we know it's wrong to worship something other than God. But how often do we think about the fact that productivity can become our idol if we aren't careful?

As I've already mentioned, there is nothing wrong with being productive and making a plan for your week. It's good to accomplish the tasks you need to do. Life *is* short, and we want to make the most of our time, gifts, talents, and energy in order to serve others and God while we are here on this earth.

If your level of productivity and busyness has absorbed your heart and mind and you have begun to believe that your usefulness on this earth has to do with how much you can get done, productivity may have become your idol. If you get angry at others for disrupting your tasks, if you feel like you must multitask everything, and if you get increasingly inflexible with any change of plans, it's possible that productivity might be the god you serve. Another sign that productivity may be your idol is if you are not doing well at taking care of yourself (or are in poor health) and you refuse to take rests or leisure time because it will take you away from your planned work.

God does not desire for us to be lazy; He is very clear about that in the Bible, especially in Proverbs 13:4, which says, "A sluggard's appetite is never filled, but the desires of the diligent are fully satisfied" (NIV). Though He warns us against laziness, He also does not want us to be completely caught up in something else so that our time and service to Him suffer. "Look carefully then how you walk, not as unwise but as wise, making the best use of the time, because the days are evil" (Eph. 5:15–16).

Take a little time to consider the possibility that productivity has become your idol. If reading this has opened your eyes to that fact, be sure to stop and pray, asking God for His forgiveness and direction.

A Time to Rest: The Sabbath

I want to jump to Genesis and the story of creation. God did the miraculous work of creating this earth and filling it with everything in just six days. And what did He do on the seventh day? He rested.

Do you think that an almighty and all-powerful God really needed to take a rest on the seventh day? Why would He rest if He didn't really need to?

Maybe, just maybe, He was trying to tell us something, and perhaps that thing was that it doesn't matter who you are, *rest* is important.

Whenever I talk to someone about the Sabbath, they say things like, "Oh, I don't have time to take a whole day off each week." "I can't celebrate the Sabbath because I work on Sundays." "We don't have to follow that commandment anymore; that was Mosaic law."

But Jesus said, "The Sabbath was made for man, not man for the Sabbath" (Mark 2:27).

Hang on . . . that's in the *New* Testament. That's right, it wasn't just an Old Testament thing. The Sabbath, or the Lord's Day as it came to be called, was still observed in the New Testament by Jesus and the early Christians.

I'm going to guess that when many of us think about the Sabbath, a very vivid picture comes to mind. Maybe it's a picture of family members gathered in a living room on Sunday, sitting in utter silence, reading their Bibles. The family eats premade cold foods throughout the day so they don't have to cook or make any effort at all. Anyone violating these rules will be punished and made to pray extra hard that God forgives them of their sin of lifting a finger on the Sabbath.

Do me a favor. Take that image and toss it in the trash can of your mind. Let's fill its place with something new. Jesus said, "Come to me, all who labor and are heavy laden, and I will give you rest. Take my yoke upon you, and learn from me, for I am gentle and lowly in heart, and you will find rest for your souls" (Matt. 11:28–29).

We are to come to the Lord for rest. We need the reminder that He will carry our burdens for us and that we don't need to be weighed down with them. For me, the Sabbath is a wonderful reminder that I am not simply "Merissa the writer" or "Merissa the mom," but I am a beloved child of God. Let the Sabbath be a similar reminder for you.

The more we practice Sabbath, the more of a privilege it becomes. We begin to revel in that time of rest we set aside each week, and we even look forward to it. We work hard all week, but the Sabbath reminds us that there is nothing we can do to earn God's grace or His love.

The Hebrew word for "Sabbath" is *Shabbat*, and it means to cease, to rest, or to end. In other words, the Sabbath is a time when we can stop doing what is ordinary.

As a Jewish man, Jesus observed the Sabbath, and He also showed the spiritual leaders of His time that it wasn't all they had made it out to be. Jesus showed us that the Sabbath wasn't a list of hard-and-fast rules as the Pharisees told the people, but it was a time for people to take care of themselves and do good for others. Jesus said to the Pharisees, "Which of you, having a son or an ox that has fallen into a well on a Sabbath day, will not immediately pull him out?" (Luke 14:5). He often spent His Sabbath days showing mercy and kindness to those around Him.

In the New Testament, early believers began to also use the phrase "the Lord's Day." This was the day that worshipers gathered together. This seemed to mark a change in biblical times when they moved their day of rest and Sabbath to the Lord's Day, the day they also gathered to worship the Lord.

Does your family currently observe a Sabbath or Lord's Day? If not, have you ever considered that the reason your Mondays might be such difficult days, the reason you start the week out so tired and exhausted, is because there was no day of rest in between your weeks? We are all well aware that rest refuels and reenergizes us so we can better deal with stresses later.

Legalism and the Sabbath

Many of us fall into the trap of believing that if you celebrate a day of Sabbath, you can fall into legalism. I want to be clear: Many people who observe the Sabbath do use it in a legalistic way, but it doesn't have to be that way.

Legalism occurs when we begin putting moral law above the gospel and believe we are saved by what we do. Our view of the Sabbath becomes legalistic when we believe that if we do not observe the Sabbath in a specific way, we might not get to heaven. For example, saying that you must not turn on the oven on the Sabbath is a way that humans have added to what the Bible actually says regarding the Sabbath day.

As we read in Luke 14:5, Jesus came to show us that this was wrong. There are no special things that must be done on the Sabbath besides continuing to follow God's commands.

Some people argue that since observing the Sabbath is part of the original Ten Commandments in the Old Testament, we don't have to follow it anymore. But what about the other nine commandments? Do we still follow them? Do we, as Christians, believe that it's not okay to murder or tell lies or swear? Of course we do! So why is it okay not to try to follow the fourth commandment the best we can?

The Law, or the set of rules given to us in the books of Exodus and Leviticus, has always been there to point us toward Jesus because we could never fulfill the full Law. When Jesus enters our lives and we become believers, the Ten Commandments become a description of our lives instead of just a set of instructions. We shouldn't feel that we *have* to do those things but that we *want* to do them.

How to Observe the Sabbath

While it's ideal to have a day of rest and reflection on Sunday when you are already meeting with other believers and spending time worshiping God, there will be situations in which Sunday is not going to be a day of rest for you. It's okay to choose another day to be your day of rest.

During 2019 and 2020, our family was in a pastoral internship while my husband worked through an online Bible school. During this pastoral internship, Sunday was never a day of rest for our family. The day started early and was filled with a huge checklist of things that had to be done. Knowing what our job was and that we would be unable to observe the Sabbath on Sunday, we chose Tuesday as our day of rest instead. On Tuesdays, we didn't take any calls from the church, we didn't do any work, and we spent the whole day as a family doing something we would all find relaxing. After our day of rest, we were ready to take on the rest of the week with fresh eyes, hearts, and minds.

A day of rest will look different for you than it does for me. On my day of rest, I don't mind cooking. I love to cook and bake for our family, so that is never a burden or stress for me. But perhaps your day of rest will not include cooking, and you will prepare things in advance so you and your kitchen can take the day off.

I highly recommend on all days of rest that devices, media, shopping, and any kind of competitions be put aside. Anything that causes any type of anxiety should not be allowed into your day of rest. Resting is a time for us to become healthier, have less stress, create deeper relationships, refocus, create balance and rhythm, and make time to reflect on what God has done for us.

To observe a Sabbath day, a day of rest, we are simply exercising the freedom we have in Christ. If we were slaves, we could be forced to work all the time. But we are free and allowed to give ourselves a day of rest. That day will also help to remind us of who our freedom comes from.

You might observe a day of rest in one or more of these ways:

- Do activities you find relaxing.
- Spend time with God in prayer or in His Word.
- Fellowship with other believers.
- Show compassion to others.
- Be outdoors.
- Go on walks with your family.
- Spend one-on-one time with your children.
- Take a bath.
- Read aloud to your children.
- Skip all the housework.
- Write letters.

How We Observe a Day of Rest

In my family, our day of rest still includes many of the routines outlined in other chapters of this book. We get up in the morning and follow our morning routine, but we get dressed for church instead of getting dressed for a typical day. We like to wear clothing that is a little bit nicer and that we've set aside for this day because it helps us to remember that this day is different from the rest of the week.

Once we've finished our morning routine, if we have a bit of time before church, we all sit down and read quietly before we leave. Church lasts until lunchtime, and then we are free for the afternoon. We often spend these afternoons in the company of other believers. We have a meal together or spend the afternoon just visiting. This is one of my favorite ways to spend the Sabbath because if I'm visiting with friends, I can't be doing anything else, so it's very relaxing for me.

If we don't spend the day with other believers, we either go home and have lunch or pack a picnic lunch and head off on a little family adventure. These outings are all very different and depend on the season. Some days we hike, sometimes we bike, other times we fish. We've gone to museums, on mini road trips, or to the park. Whatever we do, we always do it together as a family. We've found that doing something active or outside our home prevents us from doing any work we might be tempted to do.

We are usually home by supper, and even though I still cook on the Sabbath, we usually have leftovers or another meal that doesn't take much time to prepare. After supper, we follow our typical bedtime routine.

I know it sounds quite simple, but that's exactly the beauty of it. It doesn't take much effort to have a day of rest, but it does take a little bit of commitment.

From observing a day of rest, we've learned that just because you stop for a day, it doesn't mean you have to play catch-up the next day. We've learned that observing the Sabbath brings our family closer together and helps the following week to go smoother. We've also found that it sets a great example for those around us who are caught up in the busyness of productivity seven days a week.

Amy's Story: A Time to Rest

For years, I wrestled with rest. I knew my body and soul needed rest, yet I put off resting for the sake of being more productive. I knew from Scripture that God's design included rest, but I thought I could do fine pressing ahead and burning the midnight oil. Part of my ongoing struggle was a warped view of what rest is, and part was a lack of understanding of how rest helps me live a fuller, more productive life in the ways that matter most.

My view of rest used to be that it meant doing nothing but spending time sitting still or sleeping. Once I understood that rest can include activities that breathe life into my soul, I began to look for ways I could incorporate rest into my days. Little moments became opportunities to rest and refresh my soul. Taking an extra two minutes to gaze at the sunrise, intentionally pausing to watch my children play, and choosing to make a little time each day to do something I enjoy, like capturing nature with my camera, writing, or reading a book, all add bits of rest that leave my soul feeling rejuvenated.

Once I began to understand the benefits of rest, I started planning my days and weeks to incorporate routine times of rest. I begin each day with a time to refresh my soul by reading the Bible, praying, and journaling. Ideally, this happens before the rest of the household wakes up, but realistically, I must choose to set aside time even if rising before everyone else isn't possible. After lunchtime, we have a whole-house rest time. The youngest child naps, and the older children look at books, color, or play quietly with toys on their bed, while I read, tend to the flowers on my front porch, or do another calm, life-giving activity. When early evening rolls around, our whole family works together to tidy the house from the day's activities so that the rest of our night can be restful instead of filled with chores.

Weekly, we set aside Sunday as our day of rest. We attend church as a family in the morning, then spend the afternoon reading, enjoying nature, riding horses, or doing other activities that encourage family connection. We use Sundays to take in less email, social media, and news and to focus more on God and family.

As a homeschooling mother with a houseful of children, long chunks of time to rest are few and far between, but when I intentionally began planning routines of rest, looking for ways to incorporate life-giving activities into our days and weeks, and taking small moments to pause and enjoy life happening around me, I found I could rest while living a full, active life with my family. In fact, it is rest that makes life more enjoyable and fulfilling because I am intentionally taking the time to make the moments count.

—Amy J., Nebraska

It's Okay to Rest

I want to end this chapter by telling you again that it's okay to rest. God created a day of rest for us because He knew we were going to need it.

It's okay not to listen to the voices around you that push you into one more day of hustle or one more day of getting ahead. You know God has okayed this day of rest and He will delight in your observance of it if you ultimately use it for His glory.

I hope you will contemplate what a day of rest might mean in your life or in your family's life. What things might you do on this day that will bring you closer together and closer to God?

thirteen

Living Slower

J umping into a lifestyle that is different from the one you are currently leading can present some challenges. Even if you've already embraced a slower lifestyle, you may still find that you have some questions or that you wonder where to go from here.

Common Questions about Living Slower

Over the past decade, I've gotten thousands of questions in my inbox about living a simpler and slower lifestyle. In this chapter, you will find many of the common questions I've helped my readers deal with over the years, and I hope they will help you if you are in a similar predicament.

What if my spouse or family is not on board with living a slower lifestyle?

This is one of the most common questions I'm asked, so I understand that this may happen fairly often. Even if you and your spouse have similar personalities, they may not have had the same experience you had or read the same things you read that may have caused your desire to live a slower life. Here are my recommendations.

Before you start making big changes, sit down with your spouse or your family and explain your heartfelt feelings behind why you want to make these changes. Share with them the benefits you hope to see and how you believe they will help your family grow together.

If your spouse or family is still not on board after you talk to them, start making some changes—but make smaller, more adaptable ones at first. Do what you can with your own schedule to open up time for more fellowship, and work on building up your daily conversations with God. (Of course, talk to Him about this also and ask for His guidance!)

If you are the main cook in your home, make changes to your meals that will allow you to spend less time in the kitchen and cook healthier foods. Declutter the areas of your home that you have control over. Perhaps once your family sees the results of the changes you are making, they may be more interested, or at least less averse to making additional changes to their lifestyle.

Sometimes slow and steady is the way to go instead of jumping into things quickly, especially if members of your family are reluctant at first. But my guess is that once they ease into things, they will enjoy the changes that are being made, and you will be able to glide into slower living together.

What if I'm judged by others about living this lifestyle or doing things they think I shouldn't do?

If someone is not walking in my shoes, they don't get to decide where my steps are going. I'm always open to the opinion of others and will take it into consideration if they have valid points. But I find that people often like to speak before they think or before they consider the background of someone else.

You are the manager of your household, and if there is something you feel God is leading you to do with it, that is your decision. The only one who knows what is best for your family is you, not your neighbor, not your Aunt Sally, and not that lady with the red handbag at church.

Can you imagine if we lived our lives and made all our decisions based on the opinions of others? What a mess things would be! When God began nudging my husband and me to leave our typical American Dream lifestyle to do ministry work, do you think people thought we were smart and making a good choice? Of course not! We were judged up and down (and still are) for the decisions we made.

But we have peace about our decisions. Some were not easy, and many were decisions that others still don't understand, but we know God has led us this way for a purpose, and if God is leading our steps, we should end up in a good place.

How do I make the time to do more of the things that lead to slower living?

I often get this comment from readers: "But I could never find the time like you have!"

I didn't have the time to live this slower lifestyle either . . . until I made the time. Choices had to be made, things had to be cut, some decisions were easy and some were not. When we started to get serious about slower living, my husband was working more than full-time, and I was working full-time from home and part-time at our business, plus trying to do all the other things such as household chores, taking care of our children, homeschooling, and more. Extra time doesn't just happen; you have to make it happen.

Studies have shown that even though we believe we have less time than ever, Americans are actually working less now than we have during the previous fifty years of work history.[1] That just means we've decided to fill up our time with other things.

By removing things from your life that aren't really necessary, like an abundance of extracurricular activities, internet and TV scrolling, and other nonessentials, and paring things down to the basics, you will begin to find that you really do have the time. It just has to be reorganized and reprioritized.

How do I not feel guilty for not letting my kids participate in all the extra activities their friends are doing?

That mom guilt is strong, isn't it? We are so afraid we are going to make our kids miss out on something that we often stuff their schedules with way too many activities.

Does your child really feel passionate about piano, dance, soccer, *and* chess club? Or is their passion directed toward one thing they wish they could focus on right now, but you feel they have to have a "well-rounded" batch of activities? Why do we feel this way? Why do we feel we need to overload our children with things to do every waking minute? What happened to the days of letting boredom take over so they can explore creatively?

I am not against extra activities or classes; in fact, both of my boys are currently taking music lessons on instruments they've shown a great deal of interest in for a long time. I'm supportive of these lessons and their time spent practicing. Did I put them in these music lessons because I think they need to learn an instrument or because I think they need some kind of extracurricular activity? Absolutely not. It's not okay for us to put our children into all kinds of activities they won't enjoy. It takes up the time they have to be creative and to just be a kid, and it can cause them undue stress to have too much on their plate.

While we adults often look at children and think they have life so easy, we forget to put ourselves in their shoes. Do you remember when you were growing up and learning to discover the world for yourself? Even though your parents and friends gave you information, you wanted to be able to seek and understand for yourself whether it was really true. And I'm not talking about bad stuff here.

I can tell my children all day how to skip a rock on a lake. I can demonstrate how to throw it, I can talk about the types of stones that work best, I can give them a visual of what the stone looks like as it skips over the lake. This is a nice story for my kids, but what will they want to do with it? They will want to try it for themselves and see if it really works.

In order to let my children try things for themselves, I have to allow them the time to do it. If I'm filling up their days with an endless supply of activities when all they really want to do is figure out how to skip a rock across a lake, I've done them a disservice and disrespected their time. Childhood is so short, which I think is one of the reasons we feel we need to cram so much busywork into it. But childhood should be a time for our children to be allowed to explore the world around them, discover their own passions, and come to their own conclusions. In this way, we can raise children who have drive, are creative, and are strong in their faith because it is *theirs*, not ours.

We've chosen to cut down on some of the things we are currently doing (e.g., watching TV, playing video games, participating in an abundance of extra activities and classes). How do I break this to the kids, and how do we work through it?

Unless you find that your children respond well to a cold-turkey approach, bring these things up very slowly. If your children are teenagers, they will have to make some of these lifestyle changes on their own; you aren't going to be able to force them into it. So far, they've been living their whole life one way. It's hard to make certain changes unless they happen over time.

No matter how old your children are, take the time to talk to them about these changes and why you feel it's best to make them. If some of the things they do are hard to stop, you could offer them some kind of incentive.

In regard to extracurricular activities and lessons, ask your child which ones they are really passionate about (and not just because their friends are doing them). You can always tell them that if they stop certain activities and find that they really want to do them again, they can.

I work full-time; can I still live a slower lifestyle?

Of course! Most of us have to work full-time to be able to make a living in this day and age. Work will simply be part of your daily routine.

When you work full-time, or even part-time, the key is to be well disciplined in your daily routines and schedules. Be at work when you are at work, and don't bring the work home. This is exceptionally hard to do when you are self-employed and things sometimes cross over (especially when it's a family-run business). But as far as your time-management skills go, it's best to have your working hours and then your hours for everything else. When you leave your work at work and have a good routine and schedule, you should have plenty of time when you're not at work for the things you'd like to add into your life, such as hospitality and fellowship.

Now, if you find your work to be difficult and unfulfilling, I recommend looking for something else, if possible. Sometimes it takes a really big leap of faith to leave a job you are comfortable with and go to a job you know you will love but that is unfamiliar or will pay less.

My husband used to work full-time in insurance, and he hated it. It was a job that paid good money, but it was not at all what he wanted to do with his life. We were terrified to take the leap to be self-employed, but we knew it was best for our family's well-being, even if we didn't have that guaranteed paycheck anymore. Looking back, that was one of the best choices we ever made. Being self-employed is harder than we had imagined it would be, but it's also the very best fit for our family dynamic. Now I get to write, which is my passion and calling, my husband can provide ministry, and we can work together as a family to make the money we need to pay the bills.

I have many sentimental items; how do I minimize those possessions without feeling so attached to material things?

First, take your time deciding what to keep and what to give away. If you don't make a strong, committed decision on something and you get rid of it in haste, you might regret your decision.

Second, take pictures of things you know you don't want to physically keep but do want to keep the memory of, as

I mentioned in chapter 4. Often, our feelings are attached not to the item itself but rather to the memories surrounding that item. If you want to declutter an item but keep the memories, just take a picture that you can hold on to. Or, if you are more of a writer than a picture taker, you could also write down the memories. Both my grandma and her mother wrote down memories of their lives, and I'm much more thankful to have those writings than physical items.

You could also repurpose the items if you really want to keep them. I took scraps from a family member's aprons and put them in picture frames in my kitchen. I no longer have an item that I cannot use, but I have a fun memory whenever I look up at the wall.

Finally, you can always find a new home for the items if you don't want to keep them but want them to stay in the family. Don't force another relative to take the items if it's going to contribute to their clutter, but if someone else in your family tree is willing to hold on to some of those heirlooms when you'd rather not, let them be the keeper of those things.

Remember, our treasures are not here on this earth, but we should be storing them up in heaven. Even though we have strong memories attached to certain items, we can't take those items with us when we go. I'd much rather leave my family a legacy in a different way than in material items I want them to care for.

I've done all the things in this book to slow down, but my life still feels too fast and I feel stuck. Where do I go from here?

If you have been trying to live a slower life but still feel like things are moving too fast, or if you are unable to focus on what you want to focus on or move in the direction you know God is nudging you in, ask yourself if you've really fully committed or if you are only doing things halfway.

On another note, we also have to remember that there will be times in this life that will be a bit busier than usual. Sometimes things come up (like new babies, moves, new jobs, changes in schooling) that are unavoidable, and when they happen, they can really throw us off track. There are many different seasons in our lives, not just seasons in the year, and sometimes those seasons will be busier until they even out or until we get used to the changes we have to make to adapt. The good news is that things will even out. We will find ways to add new things into our routines and schedules, and life will get back to a simpler, slower pace.

Sit down and write out what a typical week looks like for you right now. If you've recently had a change that has made things seem chaotic again, see what adjustments can be made in order to slow things back down. If you don't feel like you've gotten to that state of slower living yet, look over that week and be honest with yourself about what changes still need to be made in your plans and activities to get you where you want to be.

I want to show my grandchildren/nieces/nephews the joys of living slower. How do I do that when they don't live with me?

Even if the children around you don't live with you, you can still expose them to the joys of living a slower life when they are with you or when you have the chance to spend time with them.

I didn't live with my grandparents when I was growing up, but their lifestyle and activities still made a huge impact on my life. I inherited a love of camping from my grandparents, and it plays a big role in my family's life today.

Don't try to be someone else when you are with children, and don't try to adapt to their lifestyle when they come to visit you. Live the simpler, slower life you love, and show that joy to the children when they are around you. Joy and happiness are infectious and will be passed on. Continue to be a positive role model in their lives, and they will look up to you, the things you do, and how you do them.

Can living slower help the environment?

For many people, a desire to help the environment is a strong force in leading them to live a simpler life. I believe God gave us the earth to live on, and it is our job to care for it the best we can out of respect for His creation.

Slower living can have an impact on the environment depending on how it is done. Our family believes in growing our own food as well as buying simple foods in bulk. This has led to a reduction of waste in our home, and our gardening practices allow us to stay away from harsh treatments or chemicals and work with the land instead of against it.

When we declutter our homes and purchase fewer items, we also help to contribute less waste. Donating items we are getting rid of allows them to be used by someone who needs them rather than ending up in a landfill. And when we find that we need fewer things, we aren't adding to the production of excess.

If you are eating at home more often and not eating as much fast food, there is much less waste in packaging. If you are staying at home more often, you may be using less gas. If you are choosing to buy secondhand when things are needed, fewer items need to be produced.

The impact of a single person can be small, but living simpler is still a step in a good direction if you are concerned about your impact on the environment.

I've decluttered, but I still feel like my home is in chaos.

You may have decluttered, but did you get rid of enough? Decluttering is a process and isn't going to happen the very first time you go through your home. When I've decluttered in order to downsize in the past, I've gone through the entire house once and then started all over again a month later. It's amazing how many more things you will find the second, third, or fourth time!

We've lived a minimalist lifestyle ever since we moved out of our three-thousand-square-foot house and into an RV several years go. In recent years, I had a big garage sale and sold so many things before we moved for an internship. When we arrived at our temporary home, I didn't unpack. I left everything in boxes unless I needed it. Before we moved back home, I was able to take two entire truckloads of stuff to the thrift store to give away. These were all boxes of stuff I never opened after the move—stuff we didn't really need. Even now, at our forever home, I constantly have a donation box going because we still find stuff we don't really need.

Decluttering is a process, and it's okay that you aren't yet satisfied with where you are at. You can always keep going and repeat the clean-out process until you are finally happy and at peace with the amount of items you have in your home.

Where do hobbies fit in with a simpler lifestyle?

I always feel like this is a loaded question and that what the person wants to ask is, "Are you telling me that I need to get rid of all my hobby and craft supplies if I want to live a simpler life?"

Of course, the answer is no.

I've found that there are many hobbies we can use to help bless others and our own families, so there is no need to cut out hobbies completely. Of course, if you have a bunch of stuff for a hobby that you don't really have a passion for, it's okay to get rid of it (no matter how much you paid for it!).

Some of my hobbies include gardening, crocheting, embroidery, fishing, off-roading, and photography. (My hubby has the same hobbies, except crocheting and embroidery.) With my gardening hobby, I produce food to feed my family. I want to grow this hobby to produce enough to feed other families as well. With my crocheting and embroidering hobbies, I make useful and beautiful things for my own home as well as for gifts to give to others. With fishing, we are able to have family togetherness and catch dinner as well. With off-roading, we are able to reach places we might not be able to get to otherwise, and I'm able to share my love of history and nature with my family in an activity we can do together that everyone enjoys. And, with photography, I'm able to share photos of ideas for simpler living with my blog readers, and my husband and I have been able to donate our photographic talents to some volunteer organizations.

Usually, hobbies are things we enjoy and that make us happy, and they can allow us to use our talents for the good of those around us. Isn't it wonderful that we can do something we enjoy to help others?

I've slowed down my lifestyle, but now I feel bored. What do I do, and what did I do wrong?

In the beginning of your journey to slower living, did you think of or remember to put together some goals? Why are you trying to live a slower life? If you haven't thought about this before and you are finding yourself bored, it's time to think on these things now.

When my husband and I began our journey to true slower living, it was extremely intentional. We didn't know all the things we would be doing or exactly how things would play out, but we knew that family togetherness was exceptionally important to us, as was following what God was clearly asking us to do. With those goals in mind, I can tell you with confidence that we are almost never bored.

If you *do* have your goals in mind but are still finding pockets of boredom in your day, it's possible that you haven't been living your simpler life long enough yet. TV and other devices make our brain think that it is being active. When we have been using them as a way to escape boredom, it can take time for our mind to adjust to a new normal.

I always look at boredom as an opportunity to be creative. If I find myself in a moment of boredom, I think, *What is something I've been wanting to do but haven't found the time to get started? Now is that moment!* (These things may range from making a new recipe to researching new methods of planting in my garden.) I also like to use moments of boredom as opportunities to learn something new, maybe by reading a book I've been wanting to read or watching a tutorial on how to make something I've been wanting to make. Also know that there is nothing wrong with rest or "boredom." As long as it doesn't turn into laziness, it's okay to stop and enjoy observing the birds out the window or to spend a few minutes taking in the sunset and reflecting on your day in prayer. Moments of stillness should not be confused for boredom and are something to be enjoyed and cherished throughout the day.

If you are experiencing true boredom, use it as an opportunity for growth, and you will never see it as a bad thing again.

How can I afford to live a simpler life?

This is one of the most wonderful things about living a simple life . . . you don't need to have money to be able to do it!

A simpler, slower lifestyle is about consuming less and not being caught up with all the things in this world. Big TVs, expensive video games, the latest fashions, large trinket collections, an overabundance of activities, the biggest house, the latest cars—all these things can be very expensive, but when you live a simpler life, you have no need for them anymore.

One of the biggest reasons we chose to live a slower lifestyle was because we knew it would be less expensive than the typical American Dream lifestyle. For a large portion of our simpler living journey, we lived in an RV. Definitely not an expensive way to live, but still a way to live a simpler, slower life. Now we live in a home that we built ourselves so we could pay cash for it. Why? Because being self-employed and in ministry doesn't exactly make you a millionaire. But it is fulfilling, and it's what we've been called to do, so we have purposely made very frugal decisions in order to do these things.

You don't need to live on forty acres next to a lake in order to have a simpler lifestyle. You don't need to drive a certain car or have a specific style of house. You can live a simpler, slower life no matter where you live and no matter what income you make.

What if I have no idea what God wants from my life?

There have been many times in my life when I've wondered what God wants from me. I always thought He wanted me to have a big family and raise a bunch of children for His glory, but then we struggled to have children. I didn't know then that His plan was for us to adopt, and I didn't know how much of a blessing that would be for us and for those around us until it happened. We don't always know what God wants from our lives, and sometimes we have to be okay with the unknown. But if you are really struggling with this question, here are some thoughts and encouragement for you.

It's easy for us to look around and compare our lives to those of others. "Just look at what he is doing. It's clear that he knows what God wants him to do!" God is absolutely concerned with the big picture of our lives, and He lives in the details as well. But we can often get hung up on thinking that every single decision in our lives must be made with a clear "sign" from God. "Oh, I see that billboard with a salad on it; that must be what God wants me to make for supper tonight." "I can't make a decision about which book to read this afternoon until God shows me which one." "I'm not sure if I should change my job or not. God isn't giving me an answer right now, so I'm waiting for a sign."

While I know that God can give us direction and talk to us to show us what to do, I also know that there are many times when He isn't going to give us an answer or show us the reason for something. We may find out the reasons for some things years down the road, and we may never know the reasons for other things until we get to heaven. In all these situations, we have to remain confident that God has a purpose and a plan for our lives. Sometimes we simply need to have the faith to go through a door and see if the next one is open or closed.

Research shows that we make an average of seventy decisions every day.[2] Don't you think God has put something in us that will allow us to make some of those decisions? For most of those trivial decisions, we are able to come up with solutions using our God-given mind.

For some decisions, we can search for a biblical reference to help us make them.

Should I wear this or that? "Women should adorn themselves in respectable apparel, with modesty and self-control, not with braided hair and gold or pearls or costly attire" (1 Tim. 2:9). Decision made. Doesn't matter if it's pink or purple, the Bible says as long as it's respectable attire, it's okay.

Should I marry this person? "Do not be unequally yoked with unbelievers. For what partnership has righteousness with lawlessness? Or what fellowship has light with darkness?" (2 Cor. 6:14).

God has given us His Word so we can make decisions based on how He wants us to live and what He wants us to do.

God has also clearly told us that we can pray about decisions we need to make. "If any of you lacks wisdom, let him ask God, who gives generously to all without reproach, and it will be given him" (James 1:5).

Have you considered seeking wise counsel on an important decision? The Bible says, "Without counsel plans fail, but with many advisers they succeed" (Prov. 15:22). And, no, this isn't about seeking the counsel of just any of your friends, this is about finding someone who is a solid believer and seeking out their advice on the matter because they will often be able to point you to the right Scripture.

As a side note, don't think God will always ask you to do something that you feel uncomfortable with. I think we often get it in our minds that God always wants to ask us to do things that will turn our world upside down and take away all the happiness from our lives. The Bible says,

> Delight yourself in the LORD,
>   and he will give you the desires of your heart.
>   (Ps. 37:4)

> For it is God who works in you, both to will and to work for his good pleasure. (Phil. 2:13)

If your desires are godly, are biblically based, and follow His commandments, God can give you the desires of your heart. Isn't that wonderful?

Are you still wondering what God wants from your life?

Stop worrying about it.

Pray in earnest.

Seek wise counsel.

Consult His Word.

Pray some more.

Trust in the LORD with all your heart,
    and do not lean on your own understanding.
In all your ways acknowledge him,
    and he will make straight your paths. (Prov. 3:5–6)

The heart of man plans his way,
    but the LORD establishes his steps. (Prov. 16:9)

For I know the plans I have for you, declares the LORD, plans for welfare and not for evil, to give you a future and a hope. (Jer. 29:11)

The LORD is good to those who wait for him,
    to the soul who seeks him. (Lam. 3:25)

I am the vine; you are the branches. Whoever abides in me and I in him, he it is that bears much fruit, for apart from me you can do nothing. (John 15:5)

And we know that for those who love God all things work together for good, for those who are called according to his purpose. (Rom. 8:28)

Afterword

I n early 2020, I made a decision that was very difficult for me to make. You see, I have issues with fully trusting anyone, but I knew it was time that I finally finish giving up control of a few more things in my life and trust that God would take care of the rest.

Our family had an opportunity to choose a path that would allow us to be quite comfortable financially, but we knew for many different reasons that it wasn't right. Even so, it was difficult to jump into the unknown and say no. After many agonizing early mornings filled with prayer and a lot of journaling (on my part), we finally concluded that it was time to make that leap. We decided to let go of the comfortable and trust that God would meet all our needs so we'd be able to do the ministry He clearly wanted us to do—without our ever asking for a paycheck or any kind of funding. In my heart, when I surrendered that full trust, I knew that if it was something God called us to, He would provide for our needs.

It hasn't been long since we made that decision, but we've already been blessed in seeing the fruit of it. Some months are a little tighter than others, but God has still provided for each and every one of our needs as we have stepped forward in faith.

Some decisions are hard to make.

It's hard to give up control, especially when we think we know how we want our lives to go.

Now that we are at the end of this book, I want to encourage you to do that very thing. Trust the plan God has for your life. Let Him help you lead your family in the way He wants them to go. Trust that His plans are even better than yours and that He will provide a way for your family to live a slower, simpler lifestyle.

Ultimately, we want to do things for His glory while we are here for a short time on this earth. As you think back to the things you've read in the previous chapters, think about whether it's possible for you or your family to do them with your current state of mind or with your current schedule.

Are you able to live the life God wants you to live with the plans you have right now?

With the activities you are doing right now?

With the stuff you have right now?

With the daily "routine" you have right now?

With the busyness you have right now?

Or does it make more sense to let some of that go, to rearrange certain areas of your life, so you find yourself having the time and motivation to follow those ultimate commands—to love God and to love others? Do you believe that if you are able to do that, God will bless your life?

I hope this book has given you insight and perhaps some drive and direction for your future. Making the decision to live a simpler, slower life seems like an easy one, but I know there's much more to it than that. Living slower is not the norm in our society. It goes against the grain, and there will be plenty of times when it will be easy to fall back into the trap of busyness once again.

I want you to remember that once you choose a simple life, it doesn't mean that from that point forward, your life will be simpler and slower. You will go through times when you will have to reevaluate your plans and schedule and make changes once again.

At the beginning of 2021, our family started a part-time business to pay the bills and to help pay for any ministry expenses we would incur. This part-time job became more than full-time before we even knew what was happening. After six months of running the business, we took a short break from it so we could step back and remember our original goals. Our lives had quickly gone from being slow and simple to being a tangled mess of busyness. Once we looked back over those original goals, it was easy to create a new plan for our business and for our family life that allowed us to slow things back down.

I'm telling you this because I want you to know that it happens. It's easy (sometimes you don't even realize it's happening) to get pulled back into the crazy, busy life the world wants us to be in, a life of distraction and chaos. But you can always choose to reset, reevaluate, and chart a new course when it seems like your life is moving in the wrong direction. The important part is that you realize what is happening so you can reroute.

Life will always throw us curveballs, and it's up to us to stay in a life of constant prayer to see what our next plan should be. You *can* live a slower, more simple life. It's not easy to go against the flow of the world, but I know you can do it.

To close, I want to use the words of the apostle Paul: "And it is my prayer that your love may abound more and more, with knowledge and all discernment" (Phil. 1:9). It is my constant prayer, reader, that you will use your discernment, and hopefully some knowledge you've gained from this book, to be able to let your love shine into your family and into this world.

—Merissa

Our Family's Favorite Recipes to Make Together

In chapter 5, I talked a lot about the simple recipes our family loves to make, and I wanted to use this section to share some of those recipes with you. Our family members have multiple food allergies, and you'd think that would mean we would have to make more complicated dishes for things to taste good.

On the contrary, we've found that simple meals are a perfect fit for our diet, not to mention our lifestyle. If you are not used to simple meals, the flavors may take some getting used to, but once you begin to allow yourself to enjoy the natural flavors of the foods that God created, it's hard to go back to anything else.

All of these recipes serve four to six people, but you can reduce or multiply as needed depending on the number of people you're cooking for.

Main Dishes

Chicken Soup

This is a winter favorite. Even though we cook it for a long time to draw out the flavor, it really needs very little hands-on time.

1–2 Tbs.	vegetable oil
2 lg.	carrots, diced
1	leek, diced
3	celery stalks, diced
4 cloves	garlic, minced
1 (15 oz.) can	artichoke hearts, drained and chopped
1 cup	cooked, shredded chicken
3 qt.	chicken broth
	salt and pepper to taste
8 oz.	noodles (optional)

In a large stockpot or Dutch oven, cook the carrots, leek, and celery on low heat in the vegetable oil for at least 15 minutes, adding more oil if necessary to keep things from sticking or burning. Then, add in the garlic and the artichoke hearts. Let everything gently cook together for another 5 minutes before adding in the chicken and the broth. Add salt and pepper to taste if needed.

Let the soup simmer on low for at least 2 hours. If you'd like to add noodles, add them 15 minutes before serving.

Easy Fried Rice

This lunch is a favorite for all the kids. I often toss in extra veggies that are in the fridge and need to be used up.

2 cups   white rice (I use jasmine or basmati)
4 cups   water
1–2 Tbs.   vegetable oil
1 sm. ('16 oz.') bag   frozen mixed vegetables (peas, carrots, etc.)
2   eggs
garlic powder
pinch of salt

In a covered saucepan, simmer the rice and water on low heat until the rice can be fluffed with a fork (about 20 minutes). Add vegetable oil to a large frying pan, and toss the vegetables in the pan with the oil over medium heat until they are warm and no longer frozen. Add the cooked rice and let everything heat together.

In a small bowl, whisk the eggs and a bit of garlic powder and salt. Pour the egg mixture over the rice and vegetables, and immediately begin stirring to mix it around. Keep stirring the mixture until you can see that the egg has cooked. Serve warm.

Meatballs with Grape Sauce

This is a great simple meal that we like to make to go with mashed potatoes or other vegetable sides.

½ cup   grape juice concentrate (You can use regular grape juice, but it may not have as much flavor.)
2 Tbs.   honey
½ cup   chicken broth
½ cup   sauerkraut
1 lb.   meatballs, cooked

In a saucepan, combine the grape juice, honey, broth, and sauerkraut. Let it all simmer together over low heat for at least 10 minutes before serving over meatballs.

I like to make my own meatballs and cook them in the oven with the sauce, reserving a little bit to pour over the top once they are done cooking.

Sides

Fried Zucchini

Fried zucchini is always a favorite summer side dish for my family. I often make this as part of a quick lunch when I have many zucchini that need to be used from the garden!

½ cup	arrowroot powder
1 tsp.	salt
½ tsp.	garlic powder
2 med.	zucchinis, sliced like large coins

In a small bowl, mix together the arrowroot powder, salt, and garlic powder. Lightly coat each piece of zucchini with the mixture, and then fry the slices on a hot nonstick or cast-iron griddle. Flip the pieces over when one side turns brown. Serve immediately after frying.

Roasted Vegetables Two Ways

We love roasted carrots, cauliflower, and really any roasted vegetable!

Regular Roasted Vegetables

2 lbs.	fresh vegetables, cut into bite-size pieces
3–4 Tbs.	olive oil
	sea salt to taste

Preheat oven to 425 degrees. Place the vegetables in a large bowl, drizzle olive oil over them until they are lightly coated, then sprinkle with sea salt. Toss the veggies until they are completely coated with the oil.

Place the vegetables in a roasting pan, and bake them for about 45 minutes. Some vegetables will need more or less time depending on the variety and the level of crunch you want them to have. You can easily double this recipe if you have a large family and more than one roasting pan.

Ranch Roasted Vegetables

1 tsp.	garlic powder
1 tsp.	dried parsley
1 tsp.	onion powder
½ tsp.	dried dill weed
1 tsp.	salt
1 tsp.	pepper
2 lbs.	fresh vegetables, cut into bite-size pieces
3–4 Tbs.	olive oil

In a small bowl, combine the garlic powder, parsley, onion powder, dill weed, salt, and pepper to make the seasoning blend.

Place the vegetables in a large bowl and drizzle olive oil over them. Sprinkle the seasoning blend over the vegetables and toss until all are coated.

Follow the directions above for baking these vegetables. (Our favorite veggie to use with the ranch seasoning is carrots. I also use this seasoning blend on chicken wings.)

Simple Coleslaw

This is one of our favorite side dishes because it tastes so fresh. It's best when it's made at least a few hours in advance, but it can be whipped together at the last minute too.

½ cup	olive oil
¼ cup	apple cider vinegar
1 Tbs.	honey
1 tsp.	garlic powder
1 tsp.	sea salt
10 cups	shredded cabbage (can be a coleslaw mix that contains, for example, red cabbage, green cabbage, and carrots)

Combine all the ingredients except the cabbage or coleslaw mix in a blender and blend the mixture for about 30 seconds or until smooth. Place the shredded cabbage or coleslaw mix in a large bowl and pour the dressing over the top. Toss until all the cabbage is covered. Refrigerate until you're ready to enjoy.

Stuffed Acorn Squash

We love this recipe in the fall or winter. To me, it tastes like a warm cinnamon roll (but a healthy one!).

1	acorn squash
1 Tbs.	coconut oil
½ cup	raisins
1 tsp.	cinnamon
2 Tbs.	maple syrup
1 sm./med.	apple, chopped
	pinch of salt

Preheat oven to 425 degrees. Cut the acorn squash in half and scoop out and discard the seeds and the stringy part of the insides. Coat the inner "meat" with coconut oil (you can melt it to spread it more easily); place the halves, skin side down, in a roasting pan in the oven; and bake for about 15 minutes.

To make the filling, combine the remaining ingredients in a bowl. When the acorn squash is finished roasting, remove it from the oven and scoop the filling into the middles of each half of the squash. Then place it back into the oven and cook for an additional 15 minutes or until the squash is soft and cooked through.

Sweet Potato Fries

In our home, we love a good sweet potato, and we make them on a regular basis. We prefer this recipe with white sweet potato varieties, but it will work with orange sweet potatoes as well.

vegetable oil or tallow for frying
2 lg. sweet potatoes
dried parsley
garlic powder
sea salt

Add two inches of vegetable oil (or tallow) to the bottom of a medium saucepan and begin heating. Peel the sweet potatoes and cut them into a French fry shape. Be sure not to cut them too thick. Once the oil is hot (test it by placing one of the pieces of potato in the oil to see if the oil starts bubbling around it), add a small batch of the potatoes to it.

Line a tray or plate with a clean towel or paper towel.

Cook the potatoes in the oil until they are golden brown, then place them on the towel-lined tray or plate.

Sprinkle the parsley, garlic, and salt over the fries to taste. Repeat the process with small batches of the remaining potatoes until you've fried all of them.

Sauces

Stir-Fry Sauce

We use this recipe so often that I never measure the ingredients anymore! This is our favorite because we usually have all the ingredients on hand and can use this sauce to coat just about any type of veggie or meat.

1 cup	beef or chicken broth
¼ cup	balsamic vinegar
1 Tbs.	blackstrap molasses
½ tsp.	garlic powder
¼ tsp.	ground ginger
1 tsp.	salt
	pepper to taste
½ cup	maple syrup
1 tsp.	arrowroot powder or cornstarch (to thicken)
⅛ cup	water

Combine all ingredients except the arrowroot powder and water in a small saucepan on the stovetop and bring to a rolling boil. Reduce heat to low and let the mixture simmer for at least 20 minutes to thicken naturally. Mix a small amount of arrowroot or cornstarch with water, and then slowly stir it into the simmering sauce until you've achieved the desired thickness. Use the sauce to coat stir-fried vegetables and meat of your choice. We just use whatever we have on hand!

Sweet-and-Sour Sauce

This sauce is so easy to make, and it's wonderful for sweet-and-sour chicken or even just for our regular stir-fry when we want a little something different.

1 (10–15 oz.) jar apricot jam
⅓ cup soy sauce (or coconut aminos)
¼ cup apple cider vinegar

Combine all ingredients together on the stovetop and simmer until the mixture thickens. Serve over stir-fried vegetables and/or meat.

Breads/Desserts

Banana Bread

I've been making this banana bread recipe for ages, and it's one of my family's favorite things to eat for breakfast, especially when it's still a little warm.

1½ cups all-purpose flour or all-purpose gluten-free flour
1¼ tsp. baking powder
½ tsp. baking soda
½ tsp. cinnamon
pinch of salt
¼ cup applesauce
2 lg. mashed bananas
¾ cup sugar
2 eggs

Preheat oven to 350 degrees. Combine all the ingredients in a large bowl and mix until no lumps remain. Pour the batter into a greased standard loaf pan. Bake for 45 to 50 minutes or until the center is set or a toothpick inserted in the center comes out clean.

Easy Cupcakes

My kids love having these cupcakes to celebrate a birthday or just for a special treat. If you want to make a vanilla version, you can leave out the cocoa powder and add a ½ cup more flour into the batter.

3 cups	all-purpose flour or all-purpose gluten-free flour
2 cups	sugar
½ cup	cocoa powder
1 tsp.	salt
2 tsp.	baking soda
1½ tsp.	vanilla
⅔ cup	vegetable oil
2 cups	water or milk or a milk alternative

Preheat oven to 350 degrees. Mix all ingredients together until there are no lumps. Pour batter into a lined 12-count cupcake tin. Bake for about 30 minutes or until a toothpick inserted into the center of one of the cupcakes comes out clean. If you plan on frosting them, make sure they are cooled completely first. Then top with your favorite frosting. I never frost mine; my kids eat them before I can!

Simple Brownies

If you are looking for a sweet treat that you can make with simple ingredients you may already have on hand, this is a great brownie recipe.

1⅓ cups   all-purpose flour or all-purpose gluten-free flour
1 cup   sugar
⅓ cup   unsweetened cocoa powder
½ tsp.   baking powder
½ tsp.   salt
½ cup   water
½ cup   vegetable oil
½ tsp.   vanilla extract

Preheat oven to 350 degrees. Combine all the ingredients in a large bowl and mix until no lumps remain. Pour the batter into a greased 8x8 baking dish. Bake for about 20 minutes or until a toothpick inserted into the center comes out clean.

If you need more brownies, you can double this recipe and bake it in a 9x13 pan for about 35 minutes or until a toothpick comes out clean. You can also add in chocolate chips, cookie pieces, or anything else you can think of for fun alternatives to the basic recipe.

Sugar Cookies

While we don't often make dessert, this recipe is one of our favorites to make on pretty much every single holiday. I've considered getting rid of my cookie cutters in the past, but thanks to this recipe, we keep them around! Keep in mind that this makes a LARGE batch of cookies so you might want to cut it in half if you aren't feeding a crowd.

1 cup   butter or buttery spread alternative, melted
2 cups   sugar
2   eggs
1½ tsp.   vanilla
5 cups   all-purpose flour or all-purpose gluten-free flour

1 tsp. salt
1 tsp. baking soda
1 cup   sour cream or yogurt (can be dairy-free
        yogurt)

Preheat oven to 400 degrees. Mix the butter and sugar in a large bowl. Add the eggs and vanilla to the sugar/butter mixture and mix well.

Add the dry ingredients to the mixture. Then add in the sour cream or yogurt. Mix until all the ingredients are blended. Roll the dough ¼ or ½ inch thick on a floured surface. Use cookie cutters to cut out shapes, then place them on a cookie sheet lined with parchment paper. Bake for about 8 minutes or until the edges are just brown.

Simple Living Journaling Topics

As you work your way through this journey to simpler and slower living, I encourage you to keep a journal. Journaling is a wonderful way to express your feelings and even to help you understand your feelings. It's also a great way to keep track of everything so one day you can look back on your journey and see exactly how far you've come or perhaps why you made the decisions you made.

Even as a writer, I have days when I just feel uninspired and not sure what to write, so I wanted to include some simple living journaling starters in this book. The journaling starters below are grouped by topic. On the days when you aren't sure what to write in your journal, pick a topic you can relate to and use one of the journaling starters to dive deep into your personal thoughts on it.

Giving God Control over Your Life

- Write about a time when your life was at a low point and you were *not* content in your situation.
- Paul wrote, "I can do all things through Christ who strengthens me" (Phil. 4:13 NKJV). What do you think he meant by this?
- Read Philippians 4:19. Do you believe this is true? Do you just know it's true, or do you actually *believe* it?
- Do you fear situations that you cannot control? How do you think you can have faith that would conquer this fear?
- Do you feel confident that whatever happens in your life is because of the will of God? Write your thoughts about this.
- Jeremiah 29:11 says God knows the plans He has for us. Do you trust that God has a plan for your life? How do you think you can discover God's plan for your life?
- Romans 8:28 says, "And we know that for those who love God all things work together for good, for those who are called according to his purpose." Do you believe that even if you make big changes in your life, God will work everything out for good? Even when some of those big changes might be scary?
- Read Proverbs 3:5–6. When it comes to making plans for your life, do you feel like you are leaning on your own understanding? How can you have more trust in the Lord?

Leading Your Family into Simpler Living

- Read Psalm 37:5. How does this verse apply to leading your family into a simpler lifestyle?
- Write a short note about each person in your family and how you think they might deal with the changes you want to make.
- Read Psalm 37:23–24. Write out a prayer for guidance to help you through this stage of your journey.
- Write another short note about each member of your family and how you think you can make this transition to slower living easier for them.
- Read Psalm 37:25–26. Write out what you hope living a simpler life will do for your children as they grow older.
- Write a letter to each member of your family about why you want to make these changes to your lifestyle and why you think doing so will be best for them and their future. Make it personal.
- Do you think your extended family will understand the changes you are making? Why or why not?
- Read Proverbs 22:6. Do you feel that right now you are raising your children the way you want them to follow when they are older? Why or why not? If not, what can be done to change things?

Materialism

- What are some material possessions that are causing you to worry right now but that you shouldn't be worrying about?

- Write a list of the things in your life you are content with and thankful for.
- Write about how having fewer possessions might change the lives of you and your family.
- Read 1 Timothy 6:17–19. What do you think these verses are telling us to do? How can you help your family to accomplish this in a loving way?
- Write down some ways you can help your children become less materialistic and more appreciative of what they have.
- Read 1 Timothy 6:11–12. From these verses, do you think living simpler will be easy? What should we be pursuing in this life instead of material things?
- Have you ever worried that your income may not be enough to keep up with your lifestyle? Why or why not?
- Write about a time when you felt pressured to buy something you didn't really want to buy.
- Write a description of what your life would look like if you weren't concerned with buying nonconsumable goods.

Fellowship and Hospitality

- Write your thoughts about how fellowship and hospitality are different.
- Read Hebrews 10:24–25. Write about a time when you neglected meeting together and how it impacted your day or week.

- Reread Hebrews 10:24. What are some things you can start doing on a regular basis to stir up others to love and good works?
- Read 1 Thessalonians 5:11. How can you encourage someone this week?
- Make a list of the people you currently feel you can have true fellowship with.
- Read Hebrews 13:2. How often do you show hospitality to strangers? If it's less than you think it should be, what are some new ways you can start doing it more?
- What does hospitality mean to you? What can it look like for your family?
- Read 1 Peter 4:9. Write about a time when you showed hospitality to someone but then "grumbled" about it. Did you complain to yourself or in front of your family?
- Read Luke 14:12–14. Think about your motives behind practicing hospitality. Do you always expect something in return when you help someone else?

Creating a Sabbath

- Do you feel that having a Sabbath day is an important part of the week? Why or why not?
- What are some activities you've done on previous Sabbath days that have been good for your family?
- Read Mark 2:27. Write your thoughts about this verse.

- Write a description of your ideal Sabbath day.
- Read Matthew 15:9. Write about how easy it is or could be to fall into a pattern of legalism when observing the Sabbath.
- Read Jeremiah 17:21. What are some "burdens" you think you should try to keep away from the Sabbath day?

Intentional Living

- Read Philippians 3:12–14. Write out your thoughts about these verses and how they may pertain to intentional living.
- Do you feel like you need to make a plan to live intentionally? Or do you feel that lives should be lived more spontaneously?
- Write out a prayer about being more intentional in your life.
- Read Ephesians 5:15–17. How do you think we can know what the will of the Lord is?
- Read Matthew 6:33. Do you find yourself seeking the kingdom of God first in your day? Why or why not?
- Read 1 Chronicles 22:13. What are some ways you get discouraged in this life? How do you think you can change to feel stronger?
- What are some actions you can take this week to live a more intentional life?

Living Quietly

- Read 1 Thessalonians 4:9–11. What does this passage tell us about how we should live? Do you feel your life reflects this right now? What are some things you can start to change to reflect this teaching?

- What is one instance in which you judged someone else this past week because they didn't live the same lifestyle as you? What should you have done instead?

- What are some ways God uses your life as an example to others, both directly and indirectly? How can you keep these in mind as you go about your "quiet" life?

- Write a prayer to God about allowing Him to use your life in accordance with His will.

- "Holiness is a process, not an achievement." Write how you feel about this statement. Keep in mind 1 Thessalonians 4:9–11 and find other verses that help to remind you of this.

Notes

Chapter 1 Our (Not So) Simple Story

1. Merissa A. Alink, *Little House Living: The Make-Your-Own Guide to a Frugal, Simple, and Self-Sufficient Life* (New York: Gallery Books, 2015).

Chapter 2 The Benefits of Living a Slower Life

1. "A Poll about Children and Weight: Crunch Time during the American Work and School Week—3pm to Bed," NPR / Robert Wood Johnson Foundation / Harvard School of Public Health, February 25, 2013, https://media.npr.org/documents/2013/feb/Children%20and%20Weight_Summary.pdf.

2. "Table 2. Time Spent in Primary Activities and Percent of the Population Engaging in Each Activity by Sex, Averages for May to December, 2019 and 2020," U.S. Bureau of Labor Statistics, Economic News Release, updated July 22, 2021, https://www.bls.gov/news.release/atus.t02.htm.

3. "Parenting in America: Outlook, Worries, Aspirations Are Strongly Linked to Financial Situation," Pew Research Center, December 17, 2015, https://www.pewsocialtrends.org/wp-content/uploads/sites/3/2015/12/2015-12-17_parenting-in-america_FINAL.pdf.

4. "Living Paycheck to Paycheck Is a Way of Life for Majority of US Workers, according to New CareerBuilder Survey: Study Highlights," CareerBuilder Press Releases, August 24, 2017, http://press.careerbuilder.com/2017-08-24-Living-Paycheck-to-Paycheck-is-a-Way-of-Life-for-Majority-of-U-S-Workers-According-to-New-CareerBuilder-Survey.

5. Lacie Glover and Shannon Bradley, "What's the Average Monthly Car Payment?," NerdWallet, August 10, 2021, https://www.nerdwallet .com/article/loans/auto-loans/average-monthly-car-payment#:~:text =The%20average%20monthly%20car%20loan,all%20up%20year%20 over%20year.

6. Joe Resendiz, "Average Credit Card Debt in America: 2021," ValuePenguin by LendingTree, updated July 9, 2021, https://www.valuepen guin.com/average-credit-card-debt.

7. Suwen Lin et al., "Social Network Structure Is Predictive of Health and Wellness," PLOS ONE, June 6, 2019, https://journals.plos.org /plosone/article?id=10.1371/journal.pone.0217264.

8. "Average Hours per Day Parents Spent Caring for and Helping Household Children as Their Main Activity," U.S. Bureau of Labor Statistics, Graphics for Economic News Releases, accessed August 24, 2021, https://www.bls.gov/charts/american-time-use/activity-by -parent.htm.

9. Victoria J. Rideout, Ulla G. Foehr, and Donald F. Roberts, *Generation M2: Media in the Lives of 8- to 18-Year-Olds* (Menlo Park: Henry J. Kaiser Family Foundation, 2010).

10. "The Common Sense Census: Media Use by Teens and Tweens in 2019," Common Sense Media, accessed August 26, 2021, https://www .commonsensemedia.org/research/the-common-sense-census-media-use -by-tweens-and-teens-2019.

11. Gloria Mark, Daniela Gudith, and Ulrich Klocke, "The Cost of Interrupted Work: More Speed and Stress," University of California, Irvine, Donald Bren School of Information and Computer Sciences, accessed August 26, 2021, https://www.ics.uci.edu/~gmark/chi08-mark.pdf.

12. Brandon T. McDaniel and Jenny S. Radesky, "Technoference: Parent Distraction with Technology and Associations with Child Behavior Problems," Child Development, May 10, 2017, https://srcd.onlinelibrary .wiley.com/doi/abs/10.1111/cdev.12822.

13. "Lost and Found: The Average American Spends 2.5 Days Each Year Looking for Lost Items Collectively Costing U.S. Households $2.7 Billion Annually in Replacement Costs," Pixie Technology Inc., May 2, 2017, https://www.prnewswire.com/news-releases/lost-and-found-the -average-american-spends-25-days-each-year-looking-for-lost-items -collectively-costing-us-households-27-billion-annually-in-replacement -costs-300449305.html.

14. Mary Macvean, "For Many People, Gathering Possessions Is Just the Stuff of Life," *Los Angeles Times*, March 21, 2014, https://www .latimes.com/health/la-xpm-2014-mar-21-la-he-keeping-stuff-20140322 -story.html.

15. "Self Storage Industry Statistics (2020)," Neighbor, December 18, 2019, https://www.neighbor.com/storage-blog/self-storage-industry -statistics.

16. "Survey Results: Americans Spend Nearly Six Hours Each Week Cleaning but Wonder, Is It Enough?," Businesswire, November 13, 2018, https://www.businesswire.com/news/home/20181113006110/en/Survey -Results-Americans-Spend-Nearly-Six-Hours-Each-Week-Cleaning-But -Wonder-Is-It-Enough.

17. "Awareness of Spiritual Gifts Is Changing," Barna, February 5, 2001, https://www.barna.com/research/awareness-of-spiritual-gifts-is -changing/.

18. In-Sue Oh, Gang Wang, and Michael K. Mount, "Validity of Observer Ratings of the Five-Factor Model of Personality Traits: A Meta-analysis," *Journal of Applied Psychology* 96, no. 4 (2011): 762–73, https:// doi.org/10.1037/a0021832.

19. Jill Anderson, "Harvard EdCast: The Benefit of Family Mealtime," Harvard Graduate School of Education, April 1, 2020, https://www.gse .harvard.edu/news/20/04/harvard-edcast-benefit-family-mealtime.

20. Anderson, "Harvard EdCast: The Benefit of Family Mealtime."

21. Jill Reedy and Susan M. Krebs-Smith, "Dietary Sources of Energy, Solid Fats, and Added Sugars among Children and Adolescents in the United States," *Journal of the American Dietetic Association* 110, no. 10 (Oct. 2010): 1477–84, https://pubmed.ncbi.nlm.nih.gov/208 69486/.

22. April Dykman, "The Financial Cost of Obesity," *Forbes*, July 27, 2011, https://www.forbes.com/sites/moneybuilder/2011/07/27/the -financial-cost-of-obesity/?sh=77a44fd5c274.

23. "President's Council on Sports, Fitness & Nutrition," Health.gov, November 1, 2020, https://www.hhs.gov/fitness/resource-center/facts-and -statistics/index.html.

24. Mohd Razali Salleh, "Life Event, Stress and Illness," *Malaysian Journal of Medical Sciences* 15, no. 4 (Oct. 2008): 9–18, https://www .ncbi.nlm.nih.gov/pmc/articles/PMC3341916/.

25. "What Is Stress?," American Institute of Stress, accessed August 27, 2021, https://www.stress.org/daily-life.

26. "What Is Stress?"

27. Jacquelyn Smith, "Here's Why Workplace Stress Is Costing Employers $300 Billion a Year," Insider, June 6, 2016, https://www.business insider.com/how-stress-at-work-is-costing-employers-300-billion-a -year-2016-6.

28. "Self-Described Christians Dominate America but Wrestle with Four Aspects of Spiritual Depth," Barna, September 13, 2011, https://

www.barna.com/research/self-described-christians-dominate-america
-but-wrestle-with-four-aspects-of-spiritual-depth/.

29. "Religion in Everyday Life," Pew Research Center, April 12, 2016, https://www.pewforum.org/2016/04/12/religion-in-everyday-life/.

30. "Americans Are Fond of the Bible, Don't Actually Read It," Lifeway Research, April 25, 2017, https://lifewayresearch.com/2017/04/25/lifeway-research-americans-are-fond-of-the-bible-dont-actually-read-it/.

31. "Sharing Faith Is Increasingly Optional to Christians," Barna, May 15, 2018, https://www.barna.com/research/sharing-faith-increasingly-optional-christians/.

32. "American Worldview Inventory 2020—At a Glance: AWVI 2020 Results—Release #8: Perceptions of Sin and Salvation," Arizona Christian University Cultural Research Center, August 4, 2020, https://www.arizonachristian.edu/wp-content/uploads/2020/08/AWVI-2020-Release-08-Perceptions-of-Sin-and-Salvation.pdf.

Chapter 5 Planning Simple, Healthy Meals

1. "Family Social Activities and Togetherness," Pew Research Center, Networked Families, October 19, 2008, https://www.pewresearch.org/internet/2008/10/19/family-social-activities-and-togetherness/.

Chapter 6 Living Seasonally

1. S. D. T. Maduwanthi and R. A. U. J. Marapana, "Induced Ripening Agents and Their Effect on Fruit Quality of Banana," International Journal of Food Science, May 2, 2019, https://www.ncbi.nlm.nih.gov/pmc/articles/PMC6521425/.

Chapter 9 Media and Technology

1. "The Dangers of Social Media and How to Avoid Them," Effectiviology, accessed September 13, 2021, https://effectiviology.com/dangers-of-social-media/.

2. "American Time Use Survey—May to December 2019 and 2020 Results," Bureau of Labor Statistics, U.S. Department of Labor, July 22, 2021, https://www.bls.gov/news.release/pdf/atus.pdf.

3. "Percentage of U.S. Population Who Currently Use Any Social Media from 2008 to 2021," Statista, accessed September 13, 2021, https://www.statista.com/statistics/273476/percentage-of-us-population-with-a-social-network-profile/#:~:text=Social%20media%20usage%20is%20one.reach%20in%20the%20previous%20year.

4. "Networked Families," Pew Research Center, October 19, 2008, https://www.pewresearch.org/internet/2008/10/19/networked-families/.

5. Lawrence Robinson and Melinda Smith, "Social Media and Mental Health," HelpGuide, updated July 2021, https://www.helpguide.org/articles/mental-health/social-media-and-mental-health.htm.

6. Jena Hilliard, "What Is Social Media Addiction?," Addiction Center, updated August 30, 2021, https://www.addictioncenter.com/drugs/social-media-addiction/.

7. Hilliard, "What Is Social Media Addiction?"

8. Ian Sample, "What Is the Internet? 13 Key Questions Answered," *The Guardian*, October 22, 2018, https://www.theguardian.com/technology/2018/oct/22/what-is-the-internet-13-key-questions-answered.

9. Sally Andrews et al., "Beyond Self-Report: Tools to Compare Estimated and Real-World Smartphone Use," PLOS ONE, October 28, 2015, https://journals.plos.org/plosone/article?id=10.1371/journal.pone.0139004.

10. Quoted in Janna Anderson and Lee Rainie, "Stories from Experts about the Impact of Digital Life: 2. The Negatives of Digital Life," Pew Research Center, July 3, 2018, https://www.pewresearch.org/internet/2018/07/03/the-negatives-of-digital-life/.

Chapter 10 Family Togetherness, Hospitality, and Fellowship

1. Cigna, *2018 Cigna U.S. Loneliness Index: Survey of 20,000 Americans Examining Behaviors Driving Loneliness in the United States*, May 2018, https://www.multivu.com/players/English/8294451-cigna-us-loneliness-survey/docs/IndexReport_1524069371598-173525450.pdf.

2. CASAColumbia, "The Importance of Family Dinners 2012," Partnership to End Addiction, September 2012, https://drugfree.org/reports/the-importance-of-family-dinners-viii/.

Chapter 12 You Have Permission to Slow Down

1. "America's #1 Health Problem," The American Institute of Stress, accessed September 17, 2021, https://www.stress.org/americas-1-health-problem.

Chapter 13 Living Slower

1. "Hours of Work in U.S. History," EH.net, accessed September 17, 2021, https://eh.net/encyclopedia/hours-of-work-in-u-s-history/.

2. Sheena Iyengar, "How to Make Choosing Easier," November 2011, TED video, https://www.ted.com/talks/sheena_iyengar_choosing_what_to_choose/transcript#t-64567.

Merissa A. Alink is the blogger behind the popular Little House Living, a website she started more than a decade ago to teach people how to live a simpler and more frugal lifestyle and which includes DIY projects, from-scratch recipes, gardening tips, and advice on modern homesteading. She and her husband, David, live in the Black Hills of South Dakota where they homeschool their three children.

Little House Living

Head to **www.littlehouseliving.com** for
recipes, DIY products, and frugal living tips.

Connect with

Merissa

Connect with

BakerBooks
Relevant. Intelligent. Engaging.

Sign up for announcements about new and upcoming titles at

BakerBooks.com/SignUp

@ReadBakerBooks